Pre-Dressing Skills

Skill Starters for Self-Help Development

by
Marsha Dunn Klein, O.T.R., M.Ed.

Illustrations by
John Furman

Therapy Skill Builders® ®
a division of
The Psychological Corporation
555 Academic Court
San Antonio, Texas 78204-2498
1-800-228-0752

About the Author

After receiving the B.S. degree in Occupational Therapy from Sargent College of Allied Health Professions at Boston University and the master's degree in Education from the University of Arizona in 1974, **Marsha Dunn Klein** worked with developmentally disabled and physically handicapped persons at the Arizona Training Program for five years. In 1980 she received the Neurodevelopmental Treatment Certificate in pediatrics and currently is in private practice as a pediatric therapist in Tucson, Arizona.

Other publications by Marsha Dunn Klein:
Pre-Writing Skills (1982)
Pre-Sign Language Motor Skills (1982)
Pre-Scissor Skills (Revised 1987)
Developmental Position Stickers (1987)
Feeding Position Stickers (1987)

With Nancy J. Harris:
Baby Position Stickers (1987)
Neonatal Position Stickers (1987)

Copyright © 1983 by

**Therapy
Skill Builders**® ®
a division of
The Psychological Corporation

555 Academic Court
San Antonio, Texas 78204-2498
1-800-228-0752

ISBN 0761646892

12 11 10

Printed in the United States of America

Contents

Introduction

Dressing and undressing skills are very much a part of everyday living for all of us. In fact, we probably take for granted our independence in this self-help area. For many people, however, the act of getting dressed or undressed can be a complicated and quite difficult process.

It is interesting to note, though, that parents of disabled children do not often list dressing as a major concern. In asking why, it seems there are generally more pressing priorities, and the small child is easy to dress. Dressing does not seem to become a concern until the child is older or until the "normal" adult has some type of accident or disease process which suddenly makes voluntary movements and daily living skills difficult.

Since dressing and undressing are activities that occur daily, either independently or with caregiver assistance, they are tasks that can be practiced regularly. If the caregivers have an understanding of various techniques, they can provide the repetition needed, and gradually can remove assistance as the dresser takes on more responsibility.

The purpose of this workbook is to provide the reader with a background in the normal developmental sequence of dressing and undressing skills and to offer suggestions in teaching approaches and techniques that can simplify the teaching process and maximize success. It offers teaching strategies, standard and adapted dressing techniques, suggestions of adaptive equipment and devices, and classroom teaching games.

Checklists and forms are provided in the workbook for assessing the person's developmental dressing skills. Task analysis and classroom activity forms are provided. All forms and checklists may be reproduced for administrative purposes.

The workbook is a self-teaching tool. It begins by listing specific objectives and ends with a test you can take to assess what you have learned. It includes periodic "probes" to bring your attention back to the information you have just read and thereby reinforce the knowledge.

Objectives

By the end of this workbook, the reader will be able to:

1. List four principles of maturation that influence the process of growth and development.

2. List eight prerequisites for dressing.

3. List the sequence strategy for the instruction for dressing, from least restrictive to most restrictive approaches.

4. Describe a standard dressing approach for:
   a. Putting on a front-button shirt
   b. Removing a front–button shirt
   c. Putting on a T-shirt
   d. Removing a T-shirt
   e. Putting on pants
   f. Removing pants
   g. Putting on shoes
   h. Removing shoes
   i. Putting on socks
   j. Removing socks
   k. Buttoning
   l. Unbuttoning
   m. Zipping
   n. Unzipping
   o. Snapping
   p. Unsnapping
   q. Buckling
   r. Unbuckling
   s. Tying
   t. Untying

5. Describe an adapted dressing approach for:
   a. Putting on a front-button shirt
   b. Removing a front-button shirt
   c. Putting on a T-shirt
   d. Removing a T-shirt
   e. Putting on pants
   f. Removing pants
   g. Putting on shoes
   h. Removing shoes
   i. Putting on socks
   j. Removing socks
   k. Tying

6. List an adaptive device for:
   a. Pants
   b. Shirts
   c. Shoes
   d. Socks
   e. Fasteners

7. List a commercially available piece of adaptive equipment used to aid in independence in:
   a. Putting on pants
   b. Putting on shoes
   c. Tying shoes
   d. Buttoning
   e. Zipping
   f. Buckling

8. Describe the teaching approach of backward chaining.

9. Describe the teaching approach of forward chaining.

10. List two dressing approaches, considerations, or hints for teaching:
    a. Shirts
    b. Pants
    c. Shoes
    d. Socks
    e. Fasteners

11. List two principles of undressing and dressing for the hemiplegic student.

12. List six handling or positioning techniques that can be helpful in relaxing or stabilizing the cerebral palsied student during dressing.

13. List five principles of undressing and dressing for the blind student.

14. List two construction considerations to be made in choosing clothing.

15. List two style considerations to be made in choosing clothing.

16. List five classroom pre-dressing activities.

17. List the components in an Individual Pre-dressing Program.

Dressing as It Relates to the Continuum
of Normal Growth and Development

A child's development will progress motorically in a reasonably predictable manner following certain general principles of development and maturation. They are:

1. Development progresses in a *cephalo-caudal* direction.
2. Development progresses in a *proximal-distal* direction.
3. Development progresses in a *medial-lateral* direction.
4. Movements are first *gross,* then *refined.*

Cephalo-Caudal Development

Development of motor control usually follows a cephalo (head) to caudal (tail) direction. Head, shoulders, and trunk control develop for sitting and reaching sooner than hip and feet control develop for walking. The beginning dressing skills of taking off a hat, sitting to pull off shoes, or balancing to push an arm in a sleeve are refined earlier than standing to put on pants or tying shoes.

Proximal-Distal Development

Movements are more controlled at the proximal joints (those closest to the midline of the body) than the distal joints (those farthest from the midline). The neck, shoulders, and hips are considered the most proximal joints. The wrist, fingers, ankles, and toes are the most distal.

The progression of arm control, therefore, develops with most control first at shoulders, then elbows, then wrists, then fingers. In dressing, children learn to use shoulders to push arms through a sleeve sooner than they learn to refine finger skills to button buttons or tie bows. The progression of leg control develops from hip to knees to ankles to toes. Therefore, children lift a leg from the hip to push it into the pant leg sooner than they learn to aim the ankle so the foot doesn't get stuck in the leg.

Medial-Lateral Development

Development of motor control — usually referring to fine motor control — progresses from a medial (closest to the midline) direction. This usually refers to the progression of hand development and is labeled from the anatomical position so the palm, when looking at the person, is facing out.

1

This relates to general grasping sequences where children voluntarily use a *whole hand grasp* initially with no thumb involvement; then grasp on the little-finger side of the hand with little and ring fingers grasping the object *(ulnar palmer grasp)*. Then they grasp the object with four fingers closing on the palm *(palmer grasp)*, to a *radial palmer grasp* where the object is obtained, still with little or no thumb involvement. The object, however, is acquired on the thumb-index-finger side of the hand with little precision. Gradually children develop a *raking grasp,* where the thumb is involved with the fingers in a "raking" action to obtain the object. Finally, a *pincer grasp* develops on the lateral side of the hand where the thumb and index and/or middle finger precisely grasp the object.

In dressing, fine motor control definitely develops with medial and palmer control first, when children merely grasp a garment to push it off or pull it on. Gradually, lateral control is refined as children develop the pincer grasp to successfully manipulate buttons or ties.

WHOLE HAND GRASP

ULNAR PALMER GRASP

PALMER GRASP

RADIAL PALMER GRASP

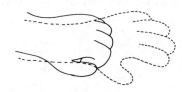

RAKING GRASP

PINCER GRASP

1. What are the four principles of maturation which influence the process of growth and development?

2. Describe an example of each principle as it relates to dressing.

3. What are the six grasps described in the progression of fine motor refinement?

Gross to Refined Development

Movements of the newborn initially are random. They are gradually directed to more precise reaching, grasping, and releasing, and eventually to refined fine motor control of fasteners. In dressing, children randomly reach out to cooperate with dressing and push the arm in the sleeve hole. Eventually, the eye-hand coordination is developed to the point of accurate aim and more controlled movements.

During the first six years of life, children develop from very dependent to more independent beings. To achieve more skill in dressing activities, they must progress through certain developmental sensory-motor stages to allow for next-step readiness. Each year they achieve skill in more of the prerequisites needed for dressing independence. A general description follows of skills achieved at each year milestone which are needed for furthered dressing independence.

Newborn

Newborns have little voluntary movements. Actions are random, lack any isolation, and are dependent on gravity and reflexes. Initially, children must be totally cared for in dressing skills.

One Year

By one year of age, children have achieved many of the developmental motor skills that serve as a foundation upon which to develop later independence. They have achieved head and neck control in all positions. They can assume a sitting position and maintain it with hands unsupported. They can pivot their body in sitting with hands freed for manipulation. They have the rotational skills to turn the head and shoulders separate from the trunk or hips. They can sit leaning backwards on arms. They can maintain balance in a sitting posture and can lift feet in that and in a supine position.

One-year-olds have learned to reach unilaterally, transfer objects hand to hand, use hands at the midline, reach forward completely, and separate movements so the arms or legs can move separate from the trunk. They can use hands bilaterally (both hands do the same thing at the same time) and have begun to use a lead-assistor pattern where one hand stabilizes and the other does the action. They have learned to adjust their posture and balance during this reaching while obtaining objects, using a pincer type grasp. They can release an object at will.

Throughout the first year, children learn to visually focus and track or follow objects, and they can perceptually see that a whole object has parts.

These skills allow children to begin to cooperate in dressing. They have the head and trunk control necessary to be comfortably balanced as they push arms or legs through sleeves and pants or play at putting a hat on and taking it off.

They can prop themselves backwards on one arm to help balance while holding up a foot for a shoe or trying to pull off socks or shoes.

Two Years

At two years, balance and equilibrium reactions have refined and children are comfortably walking and needing no support in standing. They have improved the ability to shift their weight side to side in all postures. They use more smooth rotation to attain a sitting posture. They can reach for distant objects, although still needing one arm to lean on while the other reaches. They can reach above their head with both arms alternately, without losing trunk stability; and they can reach behind their back with some exaggerated twisting. Two-year-olds can use hands consistently in a lead-assistor fashion, and they have a hand preference. Refined grasp and eye-hand coordinations continue to progress.

Children now have the prerequisite motor skills to lift arms overhead and maintain balance while pulling off an unfastened coat or sweater. By two-and-a-half they have better aim in trying to put on a sock or unbutton a large button. They can get arms behind and overhead in attempting to put on front-button shirts, and they can reach behind themselves to try to pull down elastic-waisted pants.

Three Years

Besides continuing to refine the movements previously described, children now have improved balance in sitting while reaching behind the head. They still attend to only one task at a time (for example, they stop talking while doing a dressing task). They are perceptually more aware of details of clothing and can find arm and leg holes more easily, but they do not yet consistently notice front and back.

At three and three-and-a-half, children have the ability to independently pull down pants, requiring them to appropriately reach behind the back with the arms; and they have achieved the balance to put on socks. They put on shirts, needing some assistance with T-shirts; and they have the refined coordination to button a series of buttons, zip and unzip nonseparating zippers, and unbuckle shoes or belts.

Four Years

Perceptually, by the age of four, children know right and wrong sides. Now they can do two things at once (they are able to talk and get dressed simultaneously). Fine motor coordination has progressed so they can buckle shoes or belts; zip, inserting the shank on the front of a separating zipper; and lace shoes. Behind-the-back and head coordination have improved, so they can now easily remove a T-shirt independently.

Five Years

At five, all skills of balance, equilibrium, and fine motor coordination are continuing to be refined. Children can reach behind the back with both arms now (although they need to lean forward at the trunk to do so). This enables them to close a back zipper, put on a T-shirt correctly each time, tie a knot, and generally dress unsupervised.

Six Years

Tying a bow knot and hood strings, buttoning back buttons, and snapping back snaps can be accomplished by six years.

 Name three developmental dressing skills that are achieved at each annual milestone one through six.

Developmental Pre-Dressing Checklist

It is important to have a clear understanding of "normal" stages of dressing to determine the developmental strengths and skills the child has accomplished, and to aid in choice of "next steps" for instruction.

The following pages are a Developmental Checklist for Pre-Dressing Skills, which can be reproduced as needed for administrative use, for the assessment and instruction of developmental dressing skills.

DEVELOPMENTAL PRE-DRESSING CHECKLIST

Name: _____ Date:_____

Approximate Age	Skill	Achieved Independently	Achieved with Help	Not Achieved
One Year	Cooperates in dressing			
	Holds foot up for shoe			
	Holds arm out for sleeve			
	Puts hat on head and takes it off			
	Likes to pull shoes off			
	Pushes arms through sleeves and legs through pants			
	Removes socks			
Two Years	Removes unfastened garment (coat)			
	Purposively removes shoes if laces are untied			
	Helps push down garment			
	Finds armholes in T-shirt			
Two-and-a-half years	Removes pull-down garment with elastic waist			
	Tries to put on socks			
	Puts on front-button type coat, shirt, or sweater			
	Unbuttons one large button			
Three Years	Puts on T-shirt, needing some assistance			
	Puts on shoes without fasteners (may be wrong foot)			
	Puts on socks with some difficulty turning heel			
	Independent with pull–down garment			

6

Name:_____ Date: _____

Approximate Age	Skill	Achieved Independently	Achieved with Help	Not Achieved
Three Years (continued)	Zips and unzips jacket zipper without separating or inserting shank			
	Needs assistance to remove T-shirt			
	Buttons large front buttons			
Three-and-a-half years	Finds front of clothing most of the time			
	Snaps or hooks clothing in front			
	Unzips front zipper on jacket, separating zipper			
	Puts on mittens			
	Buttons series of three or four buttons			
	Unbuckles shoe or belt			
	Puts on boots			
	Dresses with supervision			
Four Years	Removes pullover garment (T-shirt) independently			
	Buckles shoes or belt			
	Zips jacket zipper, inserting the shank			
	Puts on socks with appropriate heel placement			
	Puts on shoes with little assistance			
	Laces shoes			
	Consistently knows front and back of clothing			
Four-and-a-half years	Puts belt in loop			

DEVELOPMENTAL PRE-DRESSING CHECKLIST (continued)

Name:_____ Date: _____

Approximate Age	Skill	Achieved Independently	Achieved with Help	Not Achieved
Five Years	Puts on pullover garment correctly each time			
	Ties a knot			
	Unties tie on apron or sash			
	Dresses unsupervised			
Five-and-a-half years	Closes back zipper			
Six Years	Ties bow knot			
	Ties hood strings			
	Buttons back buttons			
	Snaps back snaps			
Eight Years	Selects clothes appropriate for weather			
Ten Years	Ties necktie			

Prerequisite Skills for Dressing

It is important to determine if students have the developmental skills and prerequisites necessary to succeed before introducing instruction for a new task. Once prerequisite skills have been assessed and skill strengths and weaknesses determined, the trainer can choose the appropriate developmental dressing skill stage, clothing type, the technique, approach, and adaptive equipment if necessary, to best suit each student's needs.

Motor Skill Prerequisites

1. *Active movement:* Students need to have the ability to move muscles actively in a voluntary fashion against gravity in order to manipulate the trunk and limbs in and out of clothing.

2. *Joint mobility:* Students should have complete range of motion in all joints in order to optimally participate in dressing and undressing activities.

3. *Coordination:* In order to stabilize joints, shift weight positions, and utilize arms, eyes, trunk, legs, and fingers together in the dressing process, students must be able to coordinate and plan motor movements in a smooth and graded fashion.

4. *Balance and equilibrium:* Students should have the ability to right themselves and maintain balance while changing postures and positions during dressing.

5. *Arm and hand control:* Students should have a hand preference, and should be able to coordinate both hands together *bilaterally* (both hands do the same thing at the same time) and in a lead-assist fashion (one hand does the lead action and the other stabilizes). Although not mandatory for dressing, reciprocal arm usage certainly helps ease speed and efficiency of dressing. In this control, the student does one action with one arm and another action with the other. An example of a bilateral dressing task is to hold a sock with two hands to pull it up. An example of a lead-assist activity would be buttoning or shoe tying. Reciprocal arm usage is noted in the opposite-arm motions used in throwing a cape around the head and over the shoulders.

6. *Reach, grasp, and release:* Students must be able to reach forward, overhead, and behind head and back to do all dressing tasks efficiently; and should be able to grasp in a refined fashion and release at will.

Sensory Skills

1. *Vision:* Students should be able to focus vision on an object, to converge and diverge focus, and to follow objects with the eyes.

2. *Perception:* Students should have learned the basic perceptual skills of coordination of the body in relationship to itself and environment, to be most proficient in dressing. They must first be able to recognize how close an object is, that two exist separately, and that there are same and different objects. They must develop a refined figure-ground development (they can figure out what is foreground and what is background). Later they will develop size and shape relationship of parts. To manipulate fasteners also requires eye-hand coordination and an internal awareness of midline.

9

3. *Tactile sensation:* Students should be able to appropriately handle the sensation of touching and manipulating a variety of different textured materials; and they must be able to have intact stereognosis, or the ability to identify objects by feel without vision. This skill is needed in feeling the armhole behind the back and in tying, zipping, or buttoning behind the back.

Body Scheme

Body part awareness and relationship of body parts: Students must have an awareness of their own body and its different parts. They must have an internal image of themselves, how their body parts relate, and where those parts are in space. They must have a perception of two sides to their body, sense the midline, and know their body's boundaries before they can perceive body parts and relationship of parts on clothing to determine how to put them on or take them off. This perceptual skill is needed to identify top from bottom and front from back on clothing.

These prerequisite skills described would optimally be present for all beginning and practiced dressers. Unfortunately, a variety of visual and perceptual and physical disabilities affect people who still must dress themselves or be dressed. Throughout this workbook, techniques of modifying teaching methods will be described to help students be independent with the skills they do have.

Name ten prerequisite skills for dressing, and give an example of how they affect dressing.

A Strategy of Instruction

The purpose of this chapter is to guide the reader in choosing a teaching strategy for the instruction of dressing. Central to any strategy chosen should be the idea that the student must succeed and that the teacher should make the *least* amount of adaptations necessary so the student will succeed. The following chapter describes consideration of techniques from least restrictive to most restrictive:

1. Use a standard technique
2. Adapt the teaching approach
3. Adapt the teaching technique
4. Adapt the teaching device
5. Adapt the equipment

Adaptations in any curriculum should only be done if a standard technique is determined inappropriate due to physical, mental, or sensory disabilities. If adaptation is needed, it usually can involve modifying the individual curriculum, changing the instructional materials, changing or modifying the physical environment, or modifying the physical presentation of the task. If the student cannot succeed in the dressing task using a standard technique and is developmentally ready and motivated to acquire the skill, you should consider an alternate technique for instruction. Remember to modify or adapt just enough for the student to succeed. Do not overmodify the task unnecessarily or use the most extreme adaptation possible at first. Minimize the changes to provide the student with the most normalized dressing experience.

It is important, therefore, initially to consider the *standard technique.* If an adapted instructional method is needed, *adapt the approach* or instructional procedure. If that adaptation does not provide success, *adapt the technique* the student uses to perform the task. Finally, consider *adapting the equipment* used. This strategy of choosing a teaching method will offer you and the student the optimum dressing experience with the most success and least restrictions.

Standard Teaching Technique

Have you ever watched three different people tie a shoe or put on a coat? Did they use three different methods? There is quite a variety of standard techniques for each dressing task. Since generally we are taught dressing skills by our parents, we learn their method of dressing. Your resultant dressing skill may be a variation on a standard method, depending on your perception of the task taught. Were you left-handed taught by a right-handed parent? Later in this workbook the author will describe standard procedures for dressing, with references to standard variations as appropriate.

Why is it important to choose instructional techniques from least restrictive to most restrictive?

Adapt the Teaching Approach

This adaptation tends to be the easiest because it requires the least amount of change. If a student could not succeed using a standard technique, perhaps an approach adaptation can make a difference. Try these:

1. Break the same activity into smaller steps
2. Change the verbal cues
3. Change the reinforcement
4. Change the environment
5. Change the criterion for success
6. Change the time of day

As adults who already have dressing skills, it is easy to teach a skill too fast and not remember how the beginning dresser needs the task broken down into small easy-to-repeat steps. Sometimes we need to listen to our verbal instruction and notice that the wording may be unclear or that the student does not know all the terms we are using. A simple change in wording can make a difference.

Are we reinforcing the student for success? Is the student motivated to complete the dressing task? This needs to be accomplished prior to instruction. If the student doesn't care about independence in dressing or a midtask reinforcement, success will be difficult to achieve.

The environment can make a difference in task success. Perhaps it is too noisy or, for the partially sighted child, too dimly or brightly lit. Perhaps brothers and sisters or classmates are distracting the student by participating in an activity nearby. Perhaps lunch is cooking and the student is smelling the food, thinking more about eating than dressing. Consider setting up the environment sensorily to be the least distracting.

Look at the criterion you set for the student to succeed. Do you expect the student to dress perfectly the first attempt, or are you allowing the desired behavior to be closely approximated?

Look seriously at the time of day you are asking the student to dress. Are you scheduling the dressing practice or exercises midmorning when other students are playing? Try to do dressing at natural dressing times and to choose times when the student is most alert and least rushed.

 List six ways to adapt the teaching approach.

Adapt the Teaching Technique

If the student would not be able to succeed with a simple adaptation in teaching approach as described, consider adapting the teaching *technique*. Use a different *method* of teaching the same task, with a different sequence of skill steps. An example of changing the teaching technique would be using the "over the head" method to remove an unbuttoned shirt rather than the standard "one arm out at a time" method. In the latter, the student slips the shirt back off one shoulder, then slips it back off the other shoulder, reaches behind the back, holds one sleeve with one hand, pulls the other arm out, then reaches in front and takes the sleeve off the other arm. This approach requires considerable shoulder movement and reaching behind the back without the assistance of vision. The "over the head" method allows more of the steps to be within vision and requires less shoulder mobility. The student reaches the back collar and grasps it to pull it over his head in one motion, then removes both arms. This change in teaching technique can mean the difference between success or no success.

Describe what is meant by adapting the teaching technique. Give an example.

Adapt the Teaching Device

If an adapted teaching technique does not allow success, you might want to consider changing the clothing or device used in the task. Consider whether a different article of clothing provides the same function and is still acceptable to the student. For example, if a student has tried to learn to tie shoes by standard approaches and variations on standard methods, and adapted teaching approaches and adapted techniques do not work, and the student has motoric difficulties in tying, consider choosing loafers, slip-on shoes, or boots. Choosing an adapted teaching device can be advantageous over adapting the equipment because it generally (1) looks more normal, (2) is less expensive, (3) is less likely to be lost or damaged, and (4) represents more normalized curriculum adaptation.

1. Describe what is meant by adapting the device. Give an example.

2. List four reasons why an adapted device may be preferable to adapted equipment.

Adapt the Teaching Equipment

If you have considered using a standard technique, adapting the approach, adapting the technique, and adapting the device and are not satisfied that any of the methods are right for the student, adapting the teaching equipment should be used only after other methods are reviewed. However, it can be the key to the independence previously denied the disabled person due to physical limitations.

The example of shoe tying can be further elaborated here. The standard technique, adapted approach, and adaptive techniques were not chosen due to physical limitations of the student. The student rejected the idea of boots or loafers because he wants to "be like the other kids" and wanted to wear jogging shoes with laces. In this case, consider shoe-matching elastic laces that look like other laces but stretch so that once they are tied, the student can use a shoe horn to get in and out of a shoe with no need for tying or untying. (Further specific pieces of adaptive equipment are illustrated and described in a later chapter.)

Remember: In choosing strategies, the least restrictive, most normalized method which affords maximum independence is the method of choice.

1. What is meant by adapting the teaching equipment? Give an example.

2. Rearrange these instructional methods into the order they should be considered for instruction: Adapt the teaching approach, use the standard technique, adapt the equipment, adapt the teaching device, adapt the teaching technique.

Dressing: Where to Begin?

1. Start dressing and undressing instruction early, to establish a routine with the student.

2. Do each dressing task the same way each time so a predictable sequenced series of steps is repeated.

3. Describe what you are doing as you are doing it with the student. For example, "Now I am putting your right foot in. Now I am putting your left leg in. Now you are standing while I am pulling up your pants."

4. As the student begins to anticipate the next step, allow time for the student to cooperate in the process. For example, pause as the student's hand is placed in the sleeve hole and allow time for him to push his arm through independently.

5. Determine the developmental skill level of the student and teach the next developmental steps for each dressing task.

6. Remember: Undressing is learned before dressing.

7. Give the student sufficient time to react.

8. Reinforce the student's efforts.

The following chapters are divided by clothing item and are further subdivided into strategy techniques for each reference.

For each garment, we have included a developmental pre-dressing checklist of the normal sequence of acquiring the dressing skill; and a *standard technique* is outlined which would be considered a way most people perform that particular dressing or undressing task.

The standard approach forms outline the *objective* to be taught, the *approximate developmental age* the student generally accomplishes the task, the *materials* needed for instruction, the *position* or positions of choice for instruction, and a *task analysis* of developmental steps needed to teach the task. The task analysis is presented in a *backward-chained* format. Backward or reverse chaining is a good step-by-step learning tool based on Skinner's Law of Chaining. In this procedure of instruction, assistance is given in the task to the last step, which the student performs, thereby successfully "completing" the task. The terminal behavior needed for the task is the *first* to be taught, and the initial behavior needed is the last. For example, the child would be assisted putting on pants all the way to the buttocks and then would be taught initially to pull up the final few inches to the waist to "complete" putting on pants. Essentially, help is given during the beginning of the procedure, and the student gradually has to complete more and more of the final steps in sequence until independence and proficiency are achieved. This method seems to work well with brain-damaged mentally retarded persons and some physically disabled patients. It may not be necessary for "normal" preschool skill instruction. In each task of the analysis, the sequence is written from last to first step in a backward-chaining approach. The illustrations shown are presented in a forward-chaining fashion for easier visualization for the reader. In the forward chaining, the first step in the task is taught first, not last.

Adapted techniques are outlined, where appropriate. These are alternate techniques which are modified to be simpler motorically for individuals with sensory-motor or learning difficulties. Remember to try an adapted technique before leaping ahead to adapted equipment.

The adapted techniques presented list the *skill* to be taught, and name the *adapted technique*, the *materials* needed, the *recommended student*, the *position* the task is to be taught in, and the *procedure*.

The adapted techniques are described in a forward-chaining approach to help the reader visualize the task. The instructional approach used can be backward or forward chaining, depending on the needs of the student.

Each garment section has a list of teaching *approaches*, *devices*, or helpful *hints* to consider when teaching the dressing or undressing skill. The approaches, or instructional procedures, can include changing the environment or the instructional setting or perhaps some of the sizes or shapes of the instructional materials. These can effectively improve instructional methods whether using a standard or adapted technique, so they are listed after techniques.

The *adapted devices* mentioned are clothing changes which can be made in the actual selection of instructional materials (for example, a loafer instead of a tie shoe).

In the following chapter (see pages 106-117), commercial adaptive equipment is mentioned and distributors' addresses are listed for easy reference. The distributors mentioned are not necessarily the only companies carrying these items. No one distributor is being recommended over the others.

Undressing and Dressing: Shirts

DEVELOPMENTAL PRE-DRESSING CHECKLIST: FRONT-BUTTON SHIRTS
(Also pajama tops, coats, sweaters)

Approximate Age	Skill	Achieved Independently	Achieved with Help	Not Achieved
One Year	Holds arm up for sleeve			
	Pushes arms through sleeve			
Two Years	Finds armhole			
	Removes unfastened shirt or shirt-type garment			
Two-and-a-half Years	Puts on front-button coat, shirt, sweater			
Three Years	Needs assistance to remove T-shirt			
	Finds front of clothing most of the time			
Four Years	Removes pullover garment independently			
	Consistently knows front and back of clothing			
Five Years	Puts shirts on carefully			

DEVELOPMENTAL PRE-DRESSING CHECKLIST: T-SHIRTS

Approximate Age	Skill	Achieved Independently	Achieved with Help	Not Achieved
One Year	Pushes arm into sleeve			
Two Years	Finds armholes			
Three Years	Puts on T-shirt (may need some assistance)			
Four Years	Knows front and back; turns clothing right side out			
Five Years	Carefully dresses			

SKILL: REMOVE A FRONT-BUTTON SHIRT

Objective: Student will remove a front-button shirt.

Approximate Developmental Age: Two years

Materials: Use a front-button shirt, jacket, sweater, or pajama top that is too large or that fits loosely.

Note: Start by unbuttoning or unzipping garment for student. Take same arm out first to help establish a routine.

Position: Sitting or standing

Task Analysis: Backward chaining. Trainer props student through entire process, leaving last part or parts for student to complete.

1. Student removes garment with one arm half-in.

2. Student removes garment with one arm in.

3. Student removes garment with one arm in and one half-in.

4. Student removes garment when pulled off shoulders.

5. Student removes garment.

SKILL: PUT ON A FRONT-BUTTON SHIRT

Objective: Student will put on a front-button shirt.

Approximate Developmental Age: Two-and-a-half years

Materials: Use a front-button shirt, jacket, sweater, or pajama top that is too large or that fits loosely.

Note: Start by unbuttoning or unzipping garment for student. Put same arm in first to establish a routine.

Position: Sitting or standing

Task Analysis: Backward chaining. Trainer props student through entire process, leaving last part or parts for student to complete.

1. Student puts on garment when one side is on the shoulder and other arm is in above elbow.

2. Student puts on garment when one side is on shoulder and other is in below elbow.

3. Student puts on garment when one side is on shoulder and other hand is in sleeve.

4. Student puts on garment when one arm is in sleeve.

5. Student puts on garment when one arm is halfway in sleeve.

6. Student puts on garment when one arm is started in sleeve.

7. Student puts on garment when guided to hold first side.

8. Student puts on garment when it is positioned near him.

SKILL: REMOVE A T-SHIRT

Objective: Student will take off a T-shirt.

Approximate
Developmental Age: Three to four years

Materials: Use a T-shirt too large for student. It should have short sleeves and a loose-fitting neck.

Position: Sitting, well balanced

Task Analysis: Backward chaining. Trainer props student through entire process, leaving last part or parts for student to complete.

1. Student removes T-shirt from head.

2. Student removes T-shirt from neck.

3. Student removes T-shirt with one arm in and one out.

4. Student removes T-shirt with one arm in and one arm half-out.

5. Student removes T-shirt when both arms are in sleeves and T-shirt has been pulled up at the shoulders.

6. Student removes T-shirt.

SKILL: REMOVE A T-SHIRT

Objective: Student will take off a T-shirt.

Approximate
Developmental Age: Three to four years

Materials: Use a T-shirt that is too large for the student.

Position: Sitting, well balanced

Task Analysis: Backward chaining. Trainer props student through entire process, leaving last part or parts for student to complete.

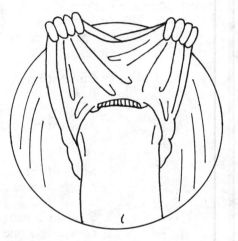

1. Student removes T-shirt from arms.

2. Student removes T-shirt from head.

3. Student pulls crossed arms over head.

4. Student grasps T-shirt on sides with crossed arms.

5. Student removes T-shirt.

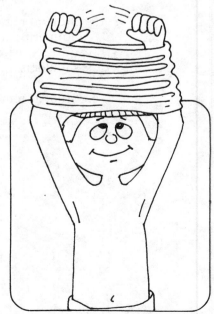

SKILL: PUT ON A T-SHIRT

Objective: Student will put on a T-shirt.

**Approximate
Developmental Age:** Three to four years

Materials: Use a T-shirt that is too large for the student. It should have short sleeves and a loose-fitting neck.

Position: Sitting, well balanced

Task Analysis: Backward chaining. Trainer props student through entire process, leaving last part or parts for student to complete.

1. Student puts on T-shirt when both arms are through sleeves (head is already in).

2. Student puts on T-shirt when one arm is through and the other is halfway in (head is already in).

3. Student puts on T-shirt when one arm is through and other hand is at the opening (head is already in).

4. Student puts on T-shirt when one arm is through (head is already in).

5. Student puts on T-shirt when it is over the head and one hand is at sleeve opening.

6. Student puts on T-shirt when placed *over* head.

7. Student puts on T-shirt when *on* head.

8. Student puts on T-shirt when placed on lap.

9. Student puts on T-shirt when handed to him.

SKILL: PUT ON A T-SHIRT

Objective: Student will put on a T-shirt.

**Approximate
Developmental Age:** Three to four years

Materials: Use a T-shirt that is too large for the student. It should have short sleeves and a loose-fitting neck.

Position: Sitting, well balanced

Task Analysis: Backward chaining. Trainer props student through entire process, leaving last part or parts to be completed by student.

1. Student pulls down T-shirt.

2. Student pulls T-shirt down on neck.

3. Student pushes both arms through sleeves at sleeve holes (either simultaneously or separately).

4. Student pushes both arms through T-shirt from the bottom to find sleeve hole.

5. Student finds bottom opening of T-shirt.

6. Student puts on T-shirt.

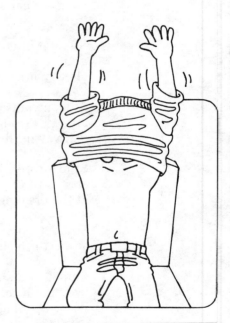

ADAPTED TECHNIQUE

Skill: Remove a front-button shirt or T-shirt

Adapted Technique: Over–the–head method

Materials: Shirt

Recommended Student: Any student

Position: Sitting or standing, well balanced

Procedure: Presented in forward chaining. Backward chaining also may be used in instruction.

1. Student reaches behind head to back of neck opening with one or both hands.

2. Student ducks head and pulls neck opening forward over head.

3. Student grasps opposite sleeve with dominant hand and pulls sleeve off arm.

4. Student removes sleeve from dominant arm by shaking or using other arm.

 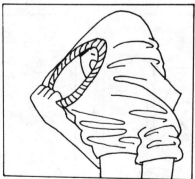 

ADAPTED TECHNIQUE

Skill: Remove a front-button shirt or T-shirt

Adapted Technique: Duck the head/sit up method

Materials: Shirt

Recommended Student: Any student, particularly the student who has limited shoulder mobility

Position: Sitting, well balanced

Procedure: Presented in forward chaining. Backward chaining also may be used in instruction.

1. Student reaches behind head to back of neck opening with one or both hands.

2. Student leans forward with head down to knees.

3. Student holds shirt neck down near knees, and sits up. The process of sitting removes the shirt.

4. Student removes both sleeves by shaking and pulling off alternate sleeve.

ADAPTED TECHNIQUE

Skill: Remove a front-button shirt

Adapted Technique: Arms-in-front method

Materials: Shirt

Recommended Student: Hemiplegic student who does not have fine motor control but can use weak arm as an assistor

Position: Sitting, well balanced

Procedure: Presented in forward chaining. Backward chaining also may be used in instruction.

1. Student pulls shirt off stronger shoulder.

2. The involved hand pulls the opposite sleeve down or forward by assisting, pushing or pulling in combination with the movement of the stronger shoulder and the trunk. Use teeth to help, when necessary.

3. The stronger arm wiggles out.

4. The stronger hand then pulls the shirt around to the front and takes sleeve off weak arm.

ADAPTED TECHNIQUE

Skill:	Put on a front-button shirt or T-shirt
Adapted Technique:	Lap/over-the-head method
Materials:	Shirt; table (optional)
Recommended Student:	Any student

This procedure is easier than many because fewer steps and fewer motions are carried out behind the back.

Position: Sitting or standing

Procedure: Presented in forward chaining. Backward chaining also may be used in instruction.

1. Student places shirt inside up with collar near trunk, on lap or table surface.

2. Student places both arms several inches in armholes.

3. Student grasps sleeves with hands over head and wiggles and shakes arms to push them completely through sleeves.

4. Student fastens fasteners.

ADAPTED TECHNIQUE

Skill: Put on a front-button shirt

Adapted Technique: Lap/over-the-head hemiplegic method

Materials: Shirt; table (optional)

Recommended Student: Hemiplegic student

Position: Sitting or standing

Procedure: Presented in forward chaining. Backward chaining also may be used in instruction.

1. Student places shirt inside up with collar near trunk, on lap or table surface.

2. Student uses stronger arm to place weak arm in sleeve hole.

3. Student pushes sleeve all the way up the weak arm above elbow near shoulder.

4. Student pushes stronger arm through sleeve.

5. Student raises stronger arm over head and wiggles and shakes it until shirt is down shoulders and on back.

6. Student fastens fasteners with stronger arm.

ADAPTED TECHNIQUE

Skill: Put on a front-button shirt

Adapted Technique: Front lap/facing-down method

Materials: Shirt; table (optional)

Recommended Student: Student who needs most of the dressing process to be in front of him to utilize vision more

Position: Sitting or standing

Procedure: Presented in forward chaining. Backward chaining also may be used for instruction.

1. Student places shirt with collar away from trunk, and face down, on lap. (A table, counter, or other flat surface can be used rather than a lap.)

2. Student puts hand underneath shirt and "walks it" toward the sleeve hole on that side.

3. Student puts hand in sleeve hole and grasps sleeve.

4. Student puts other hand underneath shirt and "walks" it toward the other sleeve hole.

5. Student puts hand in and grasps that sleeve.

6. Student lifts both arms overhead and wiggles or shakes arms so the sleeve slides down arms to shoulders.

7. Student fastens fasteners.

ADAPTED TECHNIQUE

Skill: Put on a front-button shirt

Adapted Technique: Front lap/facing-down/hemiplegic method

Materials: Shirt; table (optional)

Recommended Student: Hemiplegic student

Position: Sitting or standing

Procedure: Presented in forward chaining. Backward chaining also may be used for instruction.

1. Student places shirt with collar away from trunk, and face down on lap. (A table, counter, or other flat surface can be used rather than a lap.)

2. Student uses stronger hand to help weaker arm "slide" under the shirt to the armhole.

3. Student pushes the sleeve up above elbow near shoulder with stronger arm.

4. Student puts stronger arm in remaining sleeve.

5. Student puts stronger arm up over head and shakes and wiggles it until the shirt is down on shoulders.

6. Student uses stronger arm to take out wrinkles or bunches in shirt.

7. Student fastens fasteners with stronger arm.

ADAPTED TECHNIQUE

Skill: Put on a front-button shirt

Adapted Technique: Chair method

Materials: Shirt; chair

Recommended Student: Students with difficulty in complete shoulder mobility, or those who have perceptual difficulties visualizing the dressing sequence

Position: Sitting

Procedure: Presented in forward chaining. Backward chaining also may be used in instruction.

1. Student places (or has had placed by assistant) unbuttoned button-type shirt on the back of a chair as shown below.

2. Student sits in chair.

3. Student takes one side of the shirt off the chair and puts that arm in.

4. Student faces other side of chair, stands up, then puts other arm in shirt.

5. Student fastens shirt.

32

ADAPTED TECHNIQUE

Skill: Put on a T-shirt

Adapted Technique: Arm–head–arm method

Materials: T-shirt

Recommended Student: Any student, particularly the hemiplegic student

Position: Sitting, well balanced

Procedure: Presented in forward chaining. Backward chaining also may be used in instruction.

1. Student places T-shirt on lap, face down with neckline near knees.

2. Student uses stronger arm to help weaker arm slide inside shirt to the sleeve.

3. Student uses stronger arm to slide sleeve on the weaker arm above the elbow near the shoulder.

4. Student pulls T-shirt over neck with stronger arm.

5. Student puts stronger arm in sleeve.

6. Student pulls down the shirt with stronger arm.

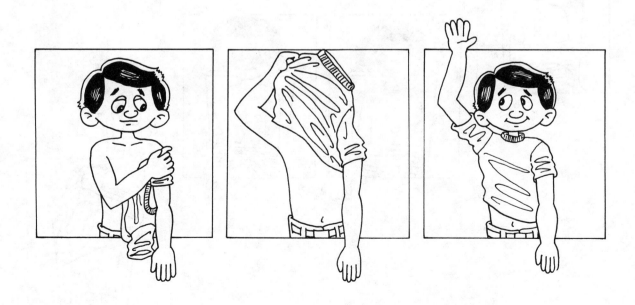

ADAPTED TECHNIQUE

Skill:	Put on a T-shirt or buttoned shirt
Adapted Technique:	Lap-neck-arm-arm method
Materials:	Shirt; table (optional)
Recommended Student:	Any student
Position:	Sitting or standing
Procedure:	Presented in forward chaining. Backward chaining also may be used in instruction.

1. Student places T-shirt or buttoned shirt on lap, face down with neckline near knees.

2. Student puts both hands in shirt.

3. Student grasps shirt at neck.

4. Student pulls neck over head.

5. Student puts both arms in.

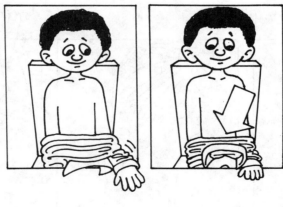
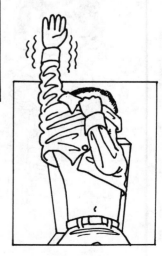

1. List the developmental sequence of taking shirts off and putting them on.

2. Describe a standard approach for putting on a front-button shirt.

3. Describe a standard approach for taking off a front-button shirt.

4. Describe a standard approach for putting on a T-shirt.

5. Describe a standard approach for taking off a T-shirt.

6. Describe two adapted techniques in taking off a shirt.

7. Describe two adapted techniques in putting on a shirt.

8. Describe two adapted techniques specifically useful for the hemiplegic student.

Approaches:

1. Be sure the student is sitting or standing comfortably with support as needed on a chair, the floor, a bed, or against a wall. The student may sit better in a corner where both walls give added support. Position the student in front of a table surface to prevent falling forward.

2. Sit next to, in front of, or directly behind the student during instruction. Guide the student through the task. For some students, it may help to sit in front of a mirror.

3. Be sure directions are clear.

4. Reinforce the student.

5. Give the student time to succeed.

6. Minimize distractions.

7. Unfasten all button-type shirts before giving them to the student.

Devices:

1. Begin shirt dressing and undressing with oversized shirts.

2. Raglan or dolman sleeves have larger arm openings than do set-in sleeves.

3. Look for shirts with easy neck openings: boat necks, horizontal crossover necks, and V-necks.

4. Capes tend to be easier to put on and take off than coats.

5. Before choosing a garment, study the student's range of motion, need for neck opening, fastener needs, sleeve style needs, and fabric restrictions.

Hints:

1. Have the student wear a mitten to prevent the fingers from getting caught as they go through the sleeve, or have the student hold a small object on the thumb while pushing the hand through.

2. If the student mobilizes with crutches, put twill tape or a patch of heavier cloth under the armhole to reinforce that area of high stress.

3. If the student tends to move a lot, a few buttons can be added to button the shirt to the pants at the waistband.

4. To help the student distinguish front from back, mark one side with a colored label or patch.

Name five approaches, devices, or hints that can optimize success in shirt dressing and undressing.

Undressing and Dressing: Pants

DEVELOPMENTAL PRE-DRESSING CHECKLIST: PANTS
(Also shorts, panties, pajamas)

Approximate Age	Skill	Achieved Independently	Achieved with Help	Not Achieved
One Year	Pushes leg through pants			
Two Years	Helps push pants down			
Two-and-a-half Years	Removes elastic-waisted pants			
Three Years	Pulls down pants independently to remove			
Three-and-a-half Years	Puts on pants (not knowing front from back)			
Four Years	Puts pants on with little assistance needed			
	Can turn clothing right side out			
Five Years	Puts pants on carefully			

SKILL: REMOVE PANTS

Objective: Student will remove pants

**Approximate
Developmental Age:** Three years

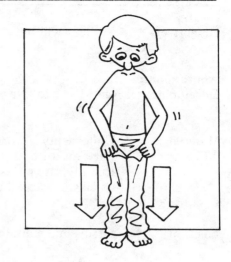

Materials: Underpants, shorts, slacks, pajama bottoms, or bathing suits can be used. Initially, use pants too large and with an elastic waistband.

Position: Standing and sitting

Task Analysis: Backward chaining. Trainer props student through entire process, leaving last part or parts for student to complete.

Note: Remove pants from the same foot. The routine will make learning easier.

1. Student removes pants when one leg is removed.

2. Student removes pants when they are pulled down to ankles.

3. Student removes pants when pulled down to knees.

4. Student removes pants when pulled down to thighs.

5. Student removes pants when pulled halfway down buttocks.

6. Student removes pants.

SKILL: PUT ON PANTS

Objective: Student will put on pants.

Approximate
Developmental Age: Four to five years

Materials: Underpants, shorts, slacks, pajama bottoms, or bathing suits can be used. Initially, use pants too large and with an elastic waistband.

Position: Sitting and standing

Task Analysis: Backward chaining. Trainer props student through entire process, leaving last part or parts for student to complete.

Note: Put pants on same leg each time. The routine will make learning easier.

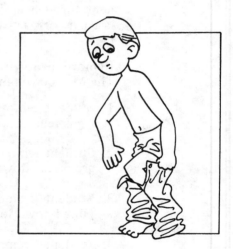

1. Student pulls on pants when pulled halfway up buttocks.

2. Student pulls on pants when just below buttocks.

3. Student pulls on pants when pulled midthigh.

4. Student pulls on pants when pulled to knees.

5. Student puts on pants when one foot is in and other is started in.

6. Student puts on pants when one foot is started in.

7. Student puts on pants when placed correctly in front of him.

8. Student puts on pants when positioned next to him.

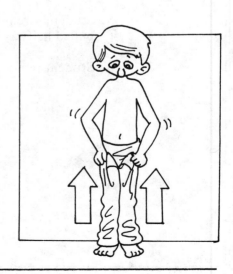

ADAPTED TECHNIQUE

Skill: Remove pants (or pull-down garment)

Adapted Technique: Sit-stand-sit method

Materials: Pants; chair; grab bar or support surface

Recommended Student: Student with limited standing balance or strength

Position: Sitting and standing supported

Procedure: Presented in forward chaining. Backward chaining also may be used for instruction.

1. Student unfastens pants in sitting position.
2. Student stands at a grab bar, counter, table, or wall for support, holding onto support with one hand.
3. Student uses one hand to lower pants below buttocks on one side.
4. Student switches hands and uses other hand to lower pants below buttocks on other side.
5. Student sits on chair.
6. Student removes pants below knees.
7. Student removes pants off ankles.
8. Student steps out of or removes pants.

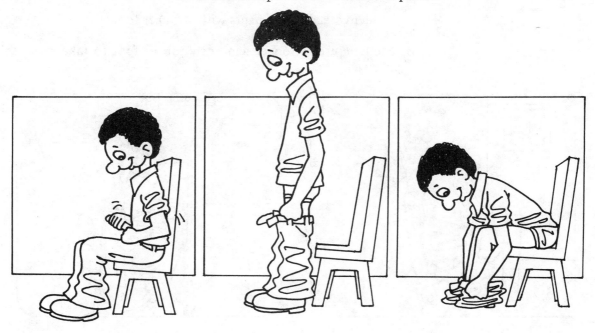

ADAPTED TECHNIQUE

Skill: Remove pants (or pull-down garment)

Adapted Technique: Sit-stand-sit hemiplegic method

Materials: Pants; chair, grab bar, counter top, table, or wall

Recommended Student: Hemiplegic student

Position: Sitting or standing supported

Procedure: Presented in forward chaining. Backward chaining also may be used for instruction.

1. Student unfastens pants in sitting position, using stronger hand.

2. Student pulls to standing, using support surface of wall, table, counter, or grab bar, to lean weaker side against while weight is still on stronger foot.

3. Student uses stronger hand to pull down pants below buttocks on both sides.

4. Student sits on chair.

5. Student uses stronger arm to remove pants below knee.

6. Student uses stronger arm to remove pants to ankle.

7. Student steps out of pants with stronger foot.

8. Student uses stronger hand or stronger foot to take pant leg off weak leg.

ADAPTED TECHNIQUE

Skill:	Remove pants (or pull-down garment)
Adapted Technique:	Sit-kneel-sit method
Materials:	Pants; chair or other support surface
Recommended Student:	Student with limited standing balance
Position:	Sitting, kneeling
Procedure:	Presented in forward chaining. Backward chaining also may be used for instruction.

1. Student unfastens pants in sitting position.

2. Student kneels in front of a chair, counter, or bed as needed for support.

3. Student uses one hand to hold support while the other hand lowers pants below buttocks.

4. Student switches hands and uses the other hand to lower pants on buttocks on other side.

5. Student repeats steps 3 and 4 as necessary.

6. Student pushes back onto chair.

7. Student removes pants below the knee.

8. Student removes pants below the ankle.

9. Student removes feet from pants.

 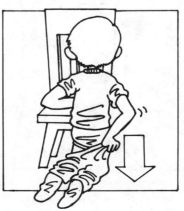 

ADAPTED TECHNIQUE

Skill: Remove pants (or pull-down garment)

Adapted Technique: Sit-kneel-sit hemiplegic method

Materials: Pants; chair, grab bar, bed, table, or wall

Recommended Student: Hemiplegic

Position: Sitting, kneeling

Procedure: Presented in forward chaining. Backward chaining also may be used for instruction.

1. Student unfastens pants in sitting position, using stronger hand.

2. Student kneels, keeping weight on stronger side.

3. Student shifts weight to weaker side, leaning on chair, bed, counter, or wall.

4. Student uses stronger hand to work pants lower than buttocks.

5. Student pushes back up onto chair.

6. Student removes pants to knees, using stronger hand (weaker arm may be wrapped around wheelchair arm).

7. Student removes pants to ankles, using stronger hand.

8. Student steps out of pants with stronger leg.

9. Student uses stronger hand or foot to take pant leg off weak leg.

  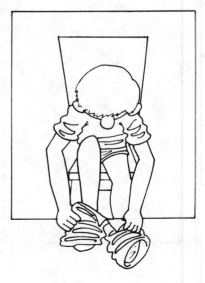

46

ADAPTED TECHNIQUE

Skill: Remove pants (or pull-down garment)

Adapted Technique: Sitting bridge method

Materials: Pants, chair

Recommended Student: Student who does not stand with enough balance to remove pants with any of the methods requiring standing or kneeling

Position: Sitting

Procedure: Presented in forward chaining. Backward chaining also may be used for instruction.

1. Student unfastens pants in sitting position.

2. Student bridges body, lifting buttocks by supporting body at feet and neck and elbows.

3. Student uses both hands to push pants below buttocks.

4. Student sits.

5. Student removes pants to knees.

6. Student removes pants to ankles.

7. Student removes feet from pants.

ADAPTED TECHNIQUE

Skill: Remove pants (or pull-down garment)

Adapted Technique: Sitting bridge hemiplegic method

Materials: Pants; chair

Recommended Student: Hemiplegic student who cannot maintain enough standing balance to remove pants with any method requiring standing or kneeling

Position: Sitting in armchair or wheelchair

Procedure: Presented in forward chaining. Backward chaining also may be used for instruction.

1. Student in sitting position unfastens pants, using stronger hand.

2. Student leans body toward weak side and bridges, lifting buttocks.

3. Student pushes pants lower than buttocks, using only the stronger hand.

4. Student sits on chair.

5. Student removes pants to knees, using stronger hand.

6. Student removes pants to ankles, using stronger hand.

7. Student steps out of pants with stronger foot and pulls pants off the other foot with the stronger hand or kicks them off with the stronger foot.

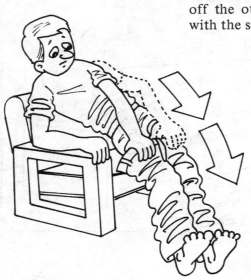

ADAPTED TECHNIQUE

Skill: Remove pants (or pull-down garment)

Adapted Technique: Supine bridge method

Materials: Pants; bed or mat

Recommended Student: Student whose sitting balance does not allow sitting during the dressing process

Position: Supine

Procedure: Presented in forward chaining. Backward chaining also may be used for instruction.

1. Student in supine position unfastens pants.

2. Student bridges with body weight at feet and shoulders.

3. Student pushes pants lower than buttocks with both hands.

4. Student either kicks and pushes pants off, or rolls from side to side while removing them.

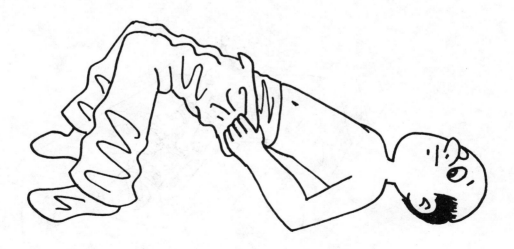

ADAPTED TECHNIQUE

Skill: Remove pants (or pull-down garment)

Adapted Technique: Supine bridge hemiplegic method

Materials: Pants; bed or mat

Recommended Student: Hemiplegic student whose sitting balance does not allow sitting during the dressing process

Position: Supine

Procedure: Presented in forward chaining. Backward chaining also may be used for instruction.

1. Student in supine position unfastens pants with stronger arm.

2. Student pushes into a bridge position with weight on weak shoulder and stronger foot.

3. Student pushes pants lower than buttocks with weak hand.

4. Student rolls toward weak side, pushes pants on side with stronger arm, then rolls farther onto weak side and uses stronger side to remove pants from weaker side.

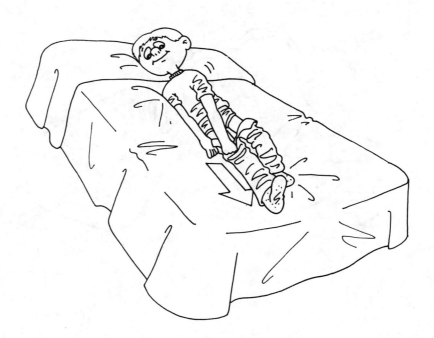

ADAPTED TECHNIQUE

Skill: Remove pants (or pull-down garment)

Adapted Technique: Supine roll method

Materials: Pants; bed or mat

Recommended Student: Student whose sitting balance does not allow sitting during the dressing process

Position: Supine

Procedure: Presented in forward chaining. Backward chaining also may be used for instruction.

1. Student in supine position unfastens pants.

2. Student, from supine, rolls to the side.

3. Student uses top arm to push down pants.

4. Student rolls to the other side, pushing down pants.

5. Student rolls from side to side, pushing pants as low as possible from that position.

6. Student kicks or pulls pants off ankles.

ADAPTED TECHNIQUE

Skill: Remove pants (or pull-down garment)

Adapted Technique: Gravity drop

Materials: Pants; table or leaning surface such as wall, grab bar, or chair

Recommended Student: Student with limited shoulder or trunk mobility and hand usage

Position: Standing

Procedure: Presented in forward chaining. Backward chaining also may be used for instruction.

1. Student stands, leaning against wall or holding onto grab bar or other support, with pants unfastened.

2. Student shifts weight back and forth while simultaneously using heel of hand or thumb in belt loops with gravity to lower pants. Student switches hands to push and support self.

3. When pants are at ankles, student steps out of them.

ADAPTED TECHNIQUE

Skill: Put on pants (or pull-on garment)

Adapted Technique: Sit-stand-sit method

Materials: Pants; chair; support (chair arm, table, wall, counter, or grab bar)

Recommended Student: Student with limited standing balance

Position: Sitting and supported standing

Procedure: Presented in forward chaining. Backward chaining also may be used for instruction.

1. Student sits on chair.

2. Student leans over and puts on pants, one ankle at a time, completely putting in foot.

3. Student pulls pants to knees.

4. Student pulls pants to above knees.

5. Student holds pants with one hand and uses the other for support while rising to a standing position.

6. Student pulls pants up over buttocks, switching support hands and pull hands as needed.

7. Student sits on chair.

8. Student fastens fasteners.

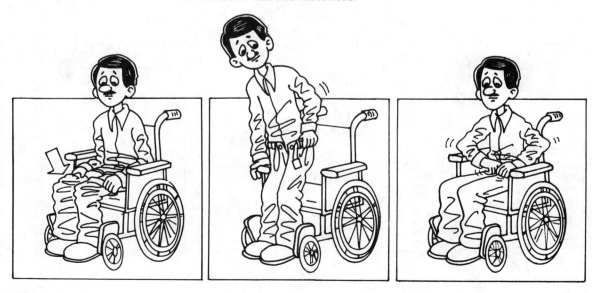

ADAPTED TECHNIQUE

Skill: Put on pants (or pull-up garment)

Adapted Technique: Sit–stand–sit hemiplegic method

Materials: Chair; pants; support surface

Recommended Student: The hemiplegic student who can move from sitting to standing, maintaining balance with minimal support

Position: Sitting, standing with support

Procedure: Presented in forward chaining. Backward chaining also may be used for instruction.

1. Student sits.

2. Student leans over and uses stronger hand to put entire weak foot into pant leg.

3. Student lifts stronger foot into pant leg.

4. Student uses stronger arm to pull up pants to knees.

5. Student uses stronger arm to pull up pants above knees.

6. Student pulls forward against a surface to stand, leaning on stronger leg and weak shoulder.

7. Student uses stronger hand to pull pants over buttocks.

8. Student sits and fastens fasteners with stronger hand.

  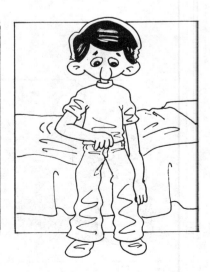

ADAPTED TECHNIQUE

Skill:	Put on pants (or pull-up garment)
Adpated Technique:	Sit-kneel-sit method
Materials:	Pants; chair; support surface
Recommended Student:	Student with limited standing balance
Position:	Sitting, kneeling
Procedure:	Presented in forward chaining. Backward chaining also may be used for instruction.

1. Student sits on chair.

2. Student leans over and puts both feet in pant legs.

3. Student pulls up pants to above knees.

4. Student moves forward and kneels with support as needed on a chair, bed, table, or grab bar.

5. Student holds onto support with one hand and pulls pants over buttocks with other.

6. Student switches hands and pulls up other side of pants.

7. Student repeats steps 5 and 6, as needed.

8. Student sits back onto chair.

9. Student fastens pants in sitting position.

 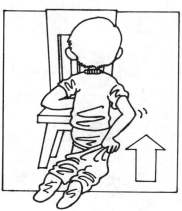 

ADAPTED TECHNIQUE

Skill:	Put on pants (or pull-up garment)
Adapted Technique:	Sit-kneel-sit hemiplegic method
Materials:	Pants; chair, grab bar, table, or other support
Recommended Student:	Hemiplegic student with precarious standing balance
Position:	Sitting, kneeling
Procedure:	Presented in forward chaining. Backward chaining also may be used for instruction.

1. Student sits on chair.

2. Student leans forward and uses stronger arm to put pant leg on weak foot.

3. Student uses stronger arm to put pant leg on stronger foot.

4. Student uses stronger arm to pull up pants above knees.

5. Student leans forward to kneeling with weight on stronger leg and weak shoulder (against wall, etc.).

6. Student pulls up pants above buttocks with stronger arm.

7. Student uses stronger leg to push up onto the chair.

8. Student uses stronger arm to fasten pants.

ADAPTED TECHNIQUE

Skill: Put on pants (or pull-up garment)

Adapted Technique: Sitting bridge method

Materials: Pants; chair

Recommended Student: Student who does not stand with enough balance to put on pants
                                      with any methods requiring standing

Position: Sitting

Procedure: Presented in forward chaining. Backward chaining also may be
                                      used for instruction.

   1. Student sits.

   2. Student leans over and puts both feet in pant legs.

   3. Student pulls pant legs to knees.

   4. Student pulls pant legs above knees.

   5. Student holds pants with both hands, bridges (buttocks up
      with weight on feet and shoulders), and pulls pants above but-
      tocks.

   6. Student sits and fastens fasteners.

ADAPTED TECHNIQUE

Skill: Put on pants (or pull-up garment)

Adapted Technique: One-side bridge-sitting method

Materials: Pants; chair

Recommended Student: Hemiplegic student who cannot maintain enough standing balance to put on pants with any method requiring standing or kneeling

Position: Sitting in armchair or wheelchair

Procedure: Presented in forward chaining. Backward chaining also may be used for instruction.

1. Student sits on chair.

2. Student leans forward to put pants leg on weak foot (or can bring foot up to lap to put pants leg on) with stronger hand.

3. Student pulls up pants leg to knee on weak side with stronger hand.

4. Student leans forward to put pants leg on stronger foot (or can bring foot up to lap to put on pants leg) with stronger hand.

5. Student pulls both sides of pant legs up above knee.

6. Student bridges with stronger foot and weak shoulder as weight points.

7. Student pulls pants above buttocks, using stronger arm.

8. Student sits.

9. Student fastens fasteners.

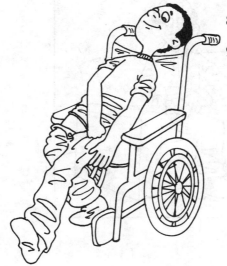

ADAPTED TECHNIQUE

Skill: Put on pants (or pull-up garment)

Adapted Technique: Supine roll method

Materials: Pants; bed or mat

Recommended Student: The student who has difficulty maintaining sitting balance while participating in dressing and undressing skills

Position: Supine

Procedure: Presented in forward chaining. Backward chaining also may be used for instruction.

1. Student is lying on one side, with hips and knees flexed.

2. Student puts pants on feet.

3. Student uses belt loops or waistband to pull up pants, and rolls from side to side until pants are completely up to waist.

4. Student fastens fasteners in supine position.

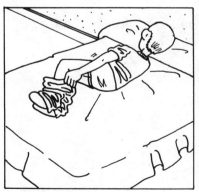 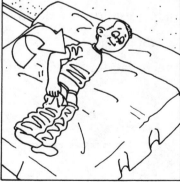 

ADAPTED TECHNIQUE

Skill: Put on pants (or pull-up garment)

Adapted Technique: Sit-lap cross-stand-sit method

Materials: Pants; chair; support surface

Recommended Student: Hemiplegic who has difficulty in the sitting balance needed to lean over

Position: Sit, stand

Procedure: Presented in forward chaining. Backward chaining also may be used for instruction.

1. Student sits on chair.
2. Student lifts weak leg with stronger arm and crosses it across lap.
3. Student uses stronger arm to put pant leg on weak foot.
4. Student lowers weak leg.
5. Student pulls up pant above knee on weak leg.
6. Student lifts stronger leg and crosses it over weak leg.
7. Student puts pant leg on stronger foot.
8. Student lowers stronger foot.
9. Student pulls up pant above knee.
10. Student stands with support as needed.
11. Student uses stronger hand to pull up pants over buttocks.
12. Student sits.
13. Student fastens fasteners with stronger arm.

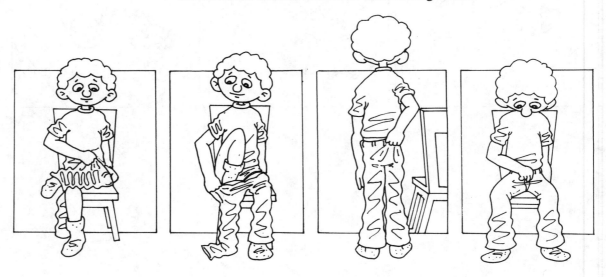

60

ADAPTED TECHNIQUE

Skill: Put on pants (or pull-up garment)

Adapted Technique: Supine roll hemiplegic method

Materials: Pants; bed or mat

Recommended Student: The student who has difficulty maintaining sitting balance while participating in dressing and undressing skills

Position: Supine

Procedure: Presented in forward chaining. Backward chaining also may be used for instruction.

1. Student rolls onto weak side.

2. Student bends legs as much as possible.

3. Student uses stronger arm to put pants on weak leg first, then on stronger leg.

4. Student rolls as much as possible toward stronger leg and pulls up pants as much as possible on weak leg.

5. Student rolls toward weak leg and pulls up pants as much as possible on stronger leg.

6. Student repeats steps 4 and 5 until pants are around waist.

7. In supine position, student uses strong arm to fasten fasteners.

ADAPTED TECHNIQUE

Skill: Put on pants (or pull-up garment)

Adapted Technique: Supine bridge hemiplegic method

Materials: Pants; chair

Recommended Student: Hemiplegic student whose sitting balance does not allow sitting during the dressing process

Position: Supine

Procedure: Presented in forward chaining. Backward chaining also may be used for instruction.

1. Student rolls to sidelying position and flexes body at hips to reach feet.

2. Student puts both feet through pants legs.

3. Student pulls up pants above knees in sidelying, first one side, then the other.

4. Student rolls to supine position and bridges with weight between feet and shoulders.

5. Student pulls pants over buttocks with one or both hands.

6. Student fastens fasteners.

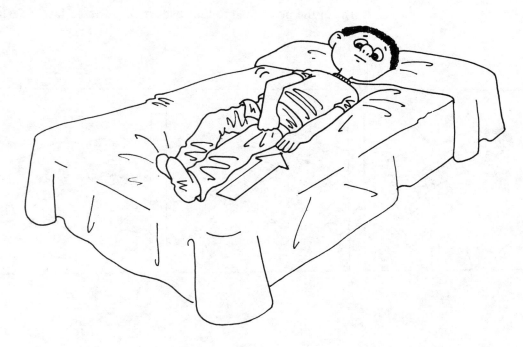

1. List the developmental sequence of putting on and removing pants.

2. Describe the standard approach for putting on pants.

3. Describe the standard approach for removing pants.

4. Describe two adapted techniques for putting on pants.

5. Describe two adapted techniques for removing pants.

6. Describe two adapted techniques that are specifically useful for the hemiplegic student.

Approaches:

1. Be sure the student is sitting or standing comfortably with support as needed on a chair, the floor, a bed, or against a wall. The student may sit better in a corner where both walls give added support.

2. Sit next to, in front of, or directly behind the student during instruction. Guide the student through the task. For some students, it may help to sit in front of a mirror.

3. Be sure directions are clear.

4. Reinforce the student.

5. Give the student time to succeed.

6. Minimize distractions.

Devices:

1. Begin with oversized pants and work toward normal-sized pants.

2. Pants without difficult fasteners generally are easier to work with. Try starting with pants with elastic waistbands. Later zippers, snaps, and buttons can be introduced.

3. Shorts, short trousers, bathing suits, and pajama bottoms often are easier to work with than long pants.

Hints:

1. Long leg seams (outer seams and inseams), zippers, or Velcro strips can be added if the student has braces or muscle tensing that makes leg movements difficult.

2. Consider the addition of extra patches at the knees for the active child who is doing considerable knee-walking or crawling. These patches can be sewn or ironed on.

3. Consider the additions of patches at the hips if needed as seam protection due to strain on pants from long leg braces.

4. Pull-loops can be sewn inside trousers waistband to help the student pull up the garment if belt loops are not already sewn on.

5. Front and back of clothing can be cued by putting a safety pin or iron-on label tape inside the pants at the back waistband.

Name five approaches, devices, or hints than can optimize success in pants undressing and dressing.

Undressing and Dressing: Socks

DEVELOPMENTAL PRE-DRESSING CHECKLIST: SOCKS

Approximate Age	Skill	Achieved Independently	Achieved with Help	Not Achieved
One Year	Holds foot up for sock			
One-and-a-half Years	Removes socks			
Two-and-a-half Years	Tries to put on socks			
Three Years	Puts on sock with difficulty turning the heel			
Four Years	Puts on socks with little assistance needed			

SKILL: REMOVE SOCKS

Objective: Student will remove socks

**Approximate
Developmental Age:** One year +

Materials: Begin with a nylon stretch sock that is too large for the student. Gradually work toward a nylon stretch sock that is the correct size. Talcum powder or cornstarch in the sock and on the foot may reduce resistance from the sock as it is being removed.

Position: Sitting, well balanced

Task Analysis: Backward chaining. Trainer props student through entire process, leaving last part or parts for student to complete.

1. Student removes sock from toes.

2. Student takes off sock from just below heel (midarch).

3. Student takes off sock from just above heel.

4. Student removes sock.

SKILL: PUT ON SOCKS

Objective: Student will put on socks

**Approximate
Developmental Age:** Two-and-a-half to four years

Materials: Begin with a nylon stretch sock that is too large for the student. Gradually work toward a nylon stretch sock that is the correct size. Talcum powder or cornstarch in the sock may reduce resistance from the sock as it is being put on.

Position: Sitting, well balanced

Task Analysis: Backward chaining. Trainer props student through entire process, leaving last part or parts for student to complete.

1. Student pulls up sock from just above heel.

2. Student pulls up sock from just below heel.

3. Student pulls up sock after toes have been started in.

4. Student puts on sock after handed to him with heel in correct position.

5. Student puts on sock with heel in correct position.

ADAPTED TECHNIQUE

Skill: Remove socks

Adapted Technique: Pull-the-toe method

Materials: Socks

Recommended Student: Any student

Position: Sitting, well balanced

Procedure: Presented in forward chaining. Backward chaining also may be used in instruction.

1. Student grasps toe of sock with one hand.

2. Student removes sock by pulling the toe of the sock one way and pulling the foot the other way.

Skill: Remove socks

Adapted Technique: Rub method

Materials: Socks

Recommended Student: Any student

Position: Sitting, well balanced

Procedure: Presented in forward chaining. Backward chaining also may be used in instruction.

1. Student pushes or rolls the sock down as far as possible, using one or two hands or rubbing sock against a mat.

2. Student finishes removing sock by grasping at the toe and pulling.

ADAPTED TECHNIQUE

Skill: Put on socks

Adapted Technique: Thumb-hook method

Materials: Socks

Recommended Student: Any student

Position: Sitting, well balanced

Procedure: Presented in forward chaining. Backward chaining also may be used in instruction.

1. Student hooks both thumbs along the side of the sock.

2. Student pulls up sock while simultaneously pushing foot into sock.

Skill: Remove socks

Adapted Technique: Thumb-hook method

Materials: Socks

Recommended Student: Any student

Position: Sitting, well balanced

Procedure: Presented in forward chaining. Backward chaining also may be used in instruction.

1. Student hooks both thumbs along the side of the sock.

2. Student pushes down sock while simultaneously pulling foot toward body.

3. Student uses one hand to remove sock from toe.

ADAPTED TECHNIQUE

Skill: Put on socks

Adapted Technique: Hemiplegic method

Materials: Socks; chair with arms; 4" x 8" high wooden box

Recommended Student: Hemiplegic student

Position: Sitting, well balanced

Procedure: Presented in forward chaining. Backward chaining also may be used in instruction.

1. Student sits on armchair and uses stronger arm to lift weaker leg onto wooden box.

2. Student leans forward to put the sock on the weaker foot first. The box helps balance when leaning to lift up stronger leg to put on sock.

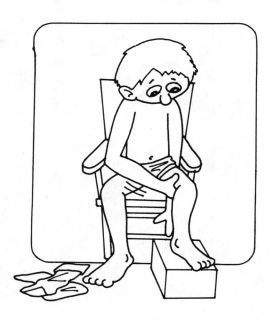

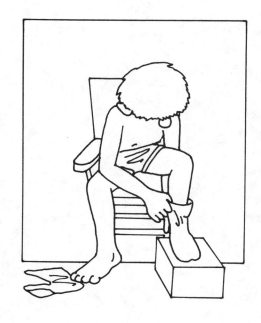

1. List the developmental sequence of putting on and taking off socks.

2. Describe a standard approach to putting on socks.

3. Describe a standard approach to taking off socks.

4. Describe an adapted technique for putting on socks.

5. Describe an adapted technique for taking off socks.

6. Describe an adapted technique that is specifically useful for the hemiplegic student.

Approaches:

1. Be sure the student is sitting comfortably with support as needed on a chair, the floor, or against a wall. The student may sit better in a corner where both walls give added support.

2. Sit next to the student during instruction, or sit behind, propping the student through the activity in front.

3. Talcum powder or cornstarch on the foot and in the sock may make it easier for the sock to slide.

4. Be sure directions are clear.

5. Reinforce the student.

6. Give the student time to succeed.

7. Minimize distractions.

Devices:

1. Begin with oversized socks. Gradually work toward normal-sized socks as proficiency increases.

2. Use socks that slide easily on the foot. Nylon socks tend to be easiest.

3. Begin initially with *tube* socks with no specific heel to position. As the student develops skills with taking off socks and putting them on, use heeled socks.

Hints:

1. If the student has trouble locating the heel, try using socks with a different-colored heel for easy visual attention.

2. If the student has difficulty with correct positioning of the sock and confuses the heel with the toe, try marking the sock; or purchase socks with toe and heel of different colors. Show the student how to align the colored toe with the toenails and different-colored sock heel with the heel of the foot.

 Name three approaches, devices, or hints that can optimize success in socks dressing and undressing.

Undressing and Dressing: Shoes

DEVELOPMENTAL PRE-DRESSING CHECKLIST: SHOES

Approximate Age	Skill	Achieved Independently	Achieved with Help	Not Achieved
One Year	Holds foot up for shoe			
	Likes to pull off shoes			
One-and-a-half Years	Tries to put on shoe			
Two Years	Purposively removes shoes if laces are untied			
Three Years	Puts on shoes without fasteners			
Four Years	Puts on shoes with little assistance needed			

SKILL: REMOVE SHOES

Objective: Student will remove shoes

**Approximate
Developmental Age:** One year +

Materials: Use a slip-on slipper, moccasin–type shoe, loafer, or tie shoe with laces removed or openly loosened.

Position: Sitting, well balanced

Task Analysis: Backward chaining. Trainer props student through entire process, leaving last part or parts for student to complete.

1. Student removes shoe when it is half-off (heel outside, toes inside) by holding heel and pulling off shoe.

2. Student removes shoe when heel is half-out.

3. Student removes a shoe (laces loose).

SKILL: PUT ON A SHOE

Objective: Student will put on a shoe

Approximate
Developmental Age: Three to four years

Materials: Use a slip-on slipper, moccasin–type shoe, loafer, or tie shoe with laces removed. Put talcum powder in shoe if sock resists in process.

Position: Sitting, well balanced, then standing

Task Analysis: Backward chaining. Trainer props student through entire process, leaving last part or parts for student to complete.

1. Student stands or leans into shoe, pushing half of heel in completely.

2. Student puts on shoe with heel out.

3. Student puts on a shoe when the toe is halfway in.

4. Student puts on a shoe when the toe is in the opening.

5. Student puts on a shoe.

SKILL: PUT A SHOE ON THE CORRECT FOOT

Objective: Student will put shoe on correct foot

**Approximate
Developmental Age:** Four years +

Materials: Initially try color-coding shoelaces with socks to help student match correct foot and shoes.

Task Analysis: Backward chaining. Trainer props student through entire process, leaving last part or parts for student to complete.

1. Student places shoe on correct foot when shown which foot.

2. Student places shoe on correct foot when shoe is placed near foot.

3. Student puts shoe on correct foot with no cues.

ADAPTED TECHNIQUE

Skill: Remove a shoe

Adapted Technique: Second-foot assist method

Materials: Shoes

Recommended Student: Any student, particularly the student who has balance difficulty and is unable to use the hands

Position: Sitting, comfortably balanced

Procedure: Presented in forward chaining. Backward chaining also may be used for instruction.

1. Student sits comfortably and places one foot (left) on floor and other foot (right) in front of it so the right heel is at the left toe.

2. Student keeps left foot on floor and pulls right foot up after left toe has caught right heel. The lifting-up process frees the right heel.

3. Student uses left foot to remove right shoe by pushing right shoe forward as right foot is being pulled back.

ADAPTED TECHNIQUE

Skill: Put on a shoe

Adapted Technique: Hemiplegic method

Materials: Shoe; chair

Recommended Student: Hemiplegic student

Position: Sitting comfortably on an armchair or straight chair, near a wall or with a table on weaker side for support

Procedure: Presented in forward chaining. Backward chaining also may be used for instruction.

Weaker Foot

1. Student uses stronger arm to lift up weaker leg across lap.

2. Student uses stronger hand to grasp side of shoe and aim it on the toe of the weaker foot.

3. Student pushes shoe on heel and completes appropriate fasteners one-handed.

4. Student lowers weaker leg to floor.

Stronger Foot

1. Student shifts weight toward the weaker side and leans body on chair arm or wall.

2. Student lifts up stronger leg across the lap so the foot can be reached by the stronger arm.

3. Student puts shoe on stronger foot.

4. Student fastens shoe with stronger arm.

5. Student lowers leg.

1. List the developmental sequence of putting on shoes and taking them off.

2. Describe a standard approach to putting on shoes.

3. Describe a standard approach to taking off shoes.

4. Describe an adapted technique to putting on shoes.

5. Describe an adapted technique to taking off shoes.

6. Describe an adapted technique that is specifically useful for the hemiplegic student.

Approaches:

1. Be sure the student is sitting comfortably with support as needed in a chair, on the floor, or against the wall.

2. Sit next to or directly behind student when demonstrating or propping the student.

3. Help the student stabilize the toe of the shoe against an immovable object to prevent the shoe from slipping as the foot is inserted.

4. Be sure directions are clear.

5. Minimize distractions.

6. Give the student time to succeed.

7. Practicing putting on shoes and taking them off is often easier if the shoe is the slip-on type of loafer or slipper.

8. Notice that some children cannot keep loafer or slipper-type shoes on due to movement or muscle patterns. They may need higher-topped laced or zippered shoes.

9. Be sure to untie and loosen the laces before practicing putting on and taking off shoes.

10. Remember that wearing socks facilitates getting tight heels into the shoe.

11. Talcum powder or cornstarch put in the shoe and on the sock may help the student slide the foot in more easily.

Devices:

1. Instead of difficult lacing or tying shoes, try loafers, slip-on shoes, shoes with zipper down the side, or shoes with Velcro D-Ring straps.

2. If lacing is difficult, often grommets can be replaced by boot-lace eyelets.

3. Use thinner and longer laces for lacing the shoe. They slide through the lace hole more easily and are less difficult to tie.

4. Have a zipper put in the shoe at a shoe repair shop. This allows for more ease in putting a shoe on a tight foot.

5. Use clip-on bow ties, if appropriate, when tying is difficult.

Hints:

1. Talk with the student's physician or physical therapist to determine optimum shoes.

2. Adaptive equipment fasteners and shoe aids may be needed to assist in pulling on the shoe and tying.

3. When students are very rough on shoes, reinforced toe caps or Swedish dip plastics can be purchased to harden the toe. Ask your local shoe specialist.

4. If the student is apt to curl the toes inside the shoe, purchase shoes with clear toes. You can see whether the toes are completely forward in the shoe. Or cut out the front of the shoe to see if the toes are completely forward. You also can reach in the shoe to use the sock to help pull the toe forward.

5. The student who curls the toes or has a tight foot or heel cord may need a shoe with a clear heel also, so the trainer can see if the heel is completely down in the shoe.

 Name four approaches and two devices that should be considered when teaching a student to put on and take off shoes.

Undressing and Dressing: Fasteners
(Buttons, Zippers, Snaps, Buckles, and Tying)

DEVELOPMENTAL PRE-DRESSING CHECKLIST: BUTTONS

Approximate Age	Skill	Achieved Independently	Achieved with Help	Not Achieved
Two to Two-and-a-half Years	Unbuttons large button			
Two-and-a-half to Three Years	Buttons large button			
Three Years	Buttons several buttons			
Five-and-a-half Years	Unbuttons back buttons			
Six to Nine Years +	Buttons back buttons			

SKILL: UNBUTTONING

Objective: Student will unbutton several buttons

Approximate Developmental Age: Two-and-a-half to three years

Materials: Use large, easy-to-handle buttons

Position: Sitting or standing

Task Analysis: Backward chaining. Trainer props student through entire learning process, leaving last part or parts for student to complete.

Note: Student will learn front buttons first, then smaller front and side buttons, and finally back buttons.

1. Student pulls halfway-removed button from buttonhole.

2. Student pulls a button from buttonhole when started.

3. Student unbuttons independently.

SKILL: BUTTONING

Objective: Student will button several buttons

Approximate Developmental Age: Three to three-and-a-half years

Materials: Use large, easy-to-handle buttons

Position: Sitting or standing

Task Analysis: Backward chaining. Trainer props student through entire learning process, leaving last part or parts for student to complete.

Note: Student will learn front buttons first, then smaller front and side buttons, and finally back buttons.

1. Student will pull the buttonhole edge of shirt over the button that is halfway through.

2. Student will pinch button and pull the buttonhole edge of shirt over the button that is just started in the hole.

3. Student will pinch button and start it through hole to button.

ADAPTED TECHNIQUE

Skill: Buttoning

Adapted Technique: One-handed method

Materials: Button shirt

Recommended Student: Any student, particularly the student who has use of only one hand

Position: Sitting or standing, well balanced

Procedure: Presented in forward chaining. Backward chaining also may be used in instruction.

1. Student grasps buttonhole between thumb and index finger.
2. Student brings buttonhole over to other side of shirt in alignment with button.
3. Student uses index and middle fingers to push button through the buttonhole toward the thumb.
4. Student buttons button completely.

Skill: Unbuttoning

Adapted Technique: One hand and assist method

Materials: Button shirt

Recommended Student: Any student, particularly the student who has use of only one hand

Position: Sitting or standing, well balanced

Procedure: Presented in forward chaining. Backward chaining also may be used in instruction.

1. Student grasps shirt near buttonhole and starts button through buttonhole with index finger and thumb.
2. Student pushes button completely through buttonhole.

DEVELOPMENTAL PRE-DRESSING CHECKLIST: ZIPPERS

Approximate Age	Skill	Achieved Independently	Achieved with Help	Not Achieved
Three Years	Unzips a nonseparating zipper			
Three-and-a-half Years	Unzips a separating zipper			
Four Years	Zips a front zipper and locks the zipper tab			
Four-and-a-half Years	Zips a separating zipper			
	Unzips back zipper			
Five-and-a-half Years	Zips back zipper			

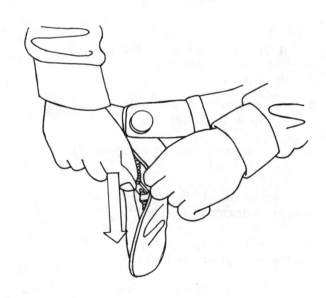

SKILL: UNZIPPING

Objective: Student will unzip a zipper

**Approximate
Developmental Age:** Three to three-and-a-half years

Materials: Use a large, easy-to-close separating jacket zipper (½" wide)

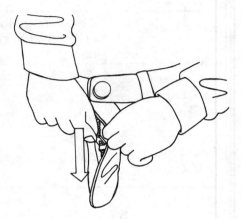

Position: Standing or sitting

Task Analysis: Backward chaining. Trainer props student through entire process, leaving the last part or parts for student to complete.

Note: *Boy:* After he can unzip a front jacket zipper, introduce front pants zippers.

Girl: After she can unzip a front jacket zipper and a side or a front pants zipper, a back dress zipper may be introduced.

1. Student unzips zipper when three-fourths unzipped.

2. Student unzips zipper when halfway unzipped.

3. Student unzips zipper when one-fourth unzipped.

4. Student unzips zipper when guided to grasp the pull tab.

5. Student unzips zipper independently.

SKILL: ZIPPING

Objective: Student will zip a zipper

**Approximate
Developmental Age:** Three to five years

Materials: Use a large, easy-to-close separating jacket zipper (½" wide)

Position: Sitting or standing

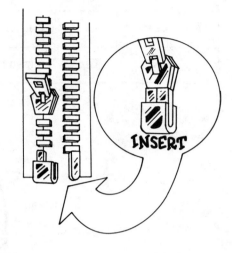

Task Analysis: Backward chaining. Trainer props student through entire process, leaving the last part or parts for student to complete.

Note: After the student can zip a separating jacket zipper with the shank already inserted into the slide bottom, introduce the insertion procedure.

1. Student zips zipper when three-fourths zipped.

2. Student zips zipper when one-fourth zipped.

3. Student zips separating zipper with shank and slide bottom already fastened, with guidance to grasp the pull tab.

4. Student holds slide bottom with one hand, is guided to insert shank into slide bottom, and zips.

5. Student zips separating zipper independently.

DEVELOPMENTAL PRE-DRESSING CHECKLIST: SNAPS

Approximate Age	Skill	Achieved Independently	Achieved with Help	Not Achieved
Two-and-a-half Years	Unsnaps front snaps			
Three Years	Closes front snaps			
Six Years	Closes back snaps			

SKILL: OPEN A SNAP

Objective: Student will open a snap

**Approximate
Developmental Age:** Two to three years

Materials: Use a shirt, vest, or jacket with easy-to-snap larger snaps.

Position: Sitting or standing

Task Analysis: Backward chaining. Trainer props student through entire process, leaving last part or parts for student to complete.

1. Student will pull both over- and under-snaps apart.

2. Student will grasp over-snap and under-snap on same snap.

3. Student will open the snap.

SKILL: CLOSE A SNAP

Objective: Student will close a snap

**Approximate
Developmental Age:** Three-and-a-half years

Materials: Use a shirt, vest, or jacket with easy-to-snap large snaps. It may help student place appropriate over- and under-snaps on a shirt if color prompts are used (for example, first over- and under-snap red, second over- and under-snap blue).

Task Analysis: Backward chaining. Trainer props student through entire process, leaving last part or parts for student to complete.

Note: *Boys:* After student snaps front shirt snaps, front pants snaps can be introduced.

Girls: After student snaps front shirt snaps, side or front snaps may be introduced.

1. Student pushes already aligned over- and under-snaps together.

2. Student holds under-snap and brings over-snap in alignment with pincer grasp.

3. Student holds under-snap and finds appropriate over-snap.

4. Student closes snap with appropriate alignment.

ADAPTED TECHNIQUE

Skill: Close a snap

Adapted Technique: One-hand method

Materials: Garment with snaps

Recommended Student: Any student, especially the hemiplegic student who does not have refined fine motor coordination

Position: Sitting or standing, well balanced

Procedure: Presented in forward chaining. Backward chaining also may be used in instruction.

1. Student grasps shirt with thumb under lower snap and index over the snap.

2. Student aligns over- and under-snaps with index finger and thumb.

3. Student closes snap.

Skill: Open a snap

Adapted Technique: One-hand method

Materials: Garment with snaps

Recommended Student: Any student, especially the hemiplegic student or one who does not have refined fine motor coordination

Position: Sitting, well balanced

Procedure: Presented in forward chaining. Backward chaining also may be used in instruction.

1. Student grasps snap with thumb and index finger as close to the snap as possible where the over- and under-snaps meet between garment layers.

2. Student pushes one finger down and one up in a lever action to open snap.

93

DEVELOPMENTAL PRE-DRESSING CHECKLIST: BUCKLES

Approximate Age	Skill	Achieved Independently	Achieved with Help	Not Achieved
Almost Four Years	Unbuckles shoes or belt			
Four Years	Buckles shoes or belt			
Four-and-a-half Years	Puts belt in pant loops			

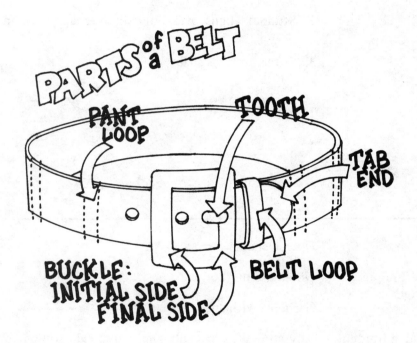

PARTS of a BELT

PANT LOOP

TOOTH

TAB END

BUCKLE: INITIAL SIDE FINAL SIDE

BELT LOOP

SKILL: UNBUCKLING

Objective: Student will unbuckle a belt

**Approximate
Developmental Age:** Three-and-a-half years

Materials: Use a large belt

Position: Standing

Task Analysis: Backward chaining. Trainer props student through entire learning process, leaving last part or parts for student to complete.

1. Student removes belt tab from buckle after tooth is unhooked.

2. Student pulls belt tab back to unhook tooth.

3. Student removes halfway-removed belt tab from final side of buckle.

4. Student removes belt tab from final side of buckle.

5. Student unbuckles belt.

SKILL: BUCKLING

Objective: Student will buckle a belt

**Approximate
Developmental Age:** Four years

Materials: Use a large belt

Position: Standing

Task Analysis: Backward chaining. Trainer props student through entire process, leaving last part or parts for student to complete.

1. Student pushes already-placed tab end of belt through pant loop.

2. Student pushes tab end of belt through pant loop.

3. Student pushes toothed belt through final side of buckle.

4. Student pushes already-aligned tooth in buckle.

5. Student pushes tooth in buckle.

6. Student pulls back already-threaded belt tab through initial side.

7. Student pulls already-started belt tab through initial side.

8. Student threads belt tab through initial buckle.

9. Student buckles independently.

DEVELOPMENTAL PRE-DRESSING CHECKLIST: TYING

Approximate Age	Skill	Achieved Independently	Achieved with Help	Not Achieved
One Year +	Unties bow on shoe			
Three Years	Tries to lace a shoe			
Four Years	Laces a shoe with difficulty			
Five Years +	Ties knot			
	Laces with ease			
Six Years	Ties bow knot			
Ten Years	Ties necktie			

SKILL: UNTYING

Objective: Student will untie a bow

**Approximate
Developmental Age:** One to three + years

Materials: Normal-sized shoelaces

Position: Sitting

Task Analysis: Backward chaining. Trainer props student through entire learning process, leaving last part or parts for student to complete.

1. Student pulls crossed laces once index finger is latched under.

2. Student latches index finger under crossed laces and pulls.

3. Student pulls one shoelace.

4. Student unties shoe.

SKILL: TYING

Objective: Student will tie a bow

**Approximate
Developmental Age:** Six years

Materials: Long, wide shoelaces; consider color-
                      coding them

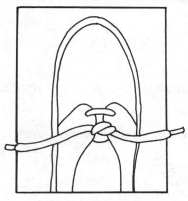

Position: Sitting

Note: It may be easier to have student prac-
                      tice the technique on a shoe in his
                      lap rather than bending to his foot.

Task Analysis: Backward chaining. Trainer props stu-
                      dent through entire learning process,
                      leaving last part or parts for student
                      to complete.

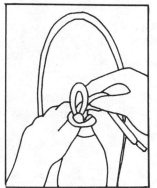

1. Student pulls both loops tight,
   once positioned with assistance.

2. Student pulls both loops tight.

3. Student pushes lace through inner
   circle with index finger toward
   thumb, making a second loop.

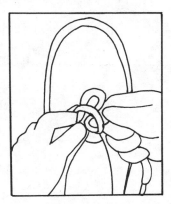

4. Student wraps lace around first
   loop.

5. Student makes a loop with one
   lace.

6. Student pulls two laces, making
   one-half knot.

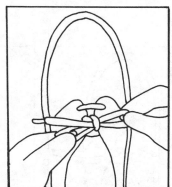

7. Student brings top lace over other
   lace and into inner circle to create
   one-half knot.

8. Student ties shoe.

ADAPTED TECHNIQUE

Skill: Tie a shoe

Adapted Technique: "Bunny ears" or "two loop tie" method

Materials: Shoe and long shoelaces

Recommended Student: Any student; however, the method requires less refined lead-assist action and fewer different steps than the standard approach

Position: A comfortable, balanced sitting posture

Procedure: Presented in forward chaining. Backward chaining also may be used for instruction.

1. Student picks up shoelaces.

2. Student crosses laces, laying them across front of shoe.

3. Student puts upper lace under the crossed laces through the cross created with the shoe in a toe-to-tongue direction.

4. Student grasps a lace in each hand and pulls tight.

5. Student makes one loop.

6. Student makes second loop with the other shoelace.

7. Student crosses loops across the front of shoe, maintaining grasp on the loops (same action as step 2).

8. Student puts upper loop under crossed laces through the triangle created with the shoe, in a toe-to-tongue direction (same action as step 3).

9. Student grasps a loop in each hand and pulls tight.

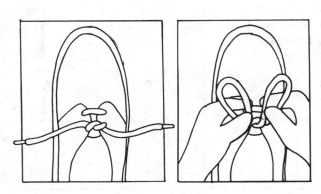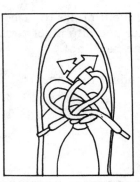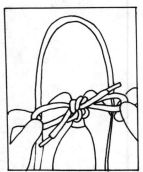

ADAPTED TECHNIQUE

Skill:	Tie a shoe
Adapted Technique:	One loop tie method
Materials:	Shoe and long shoelaces
Recommended Student:	Any student; however, the method requires fewer steps and less lead–assist hand usage than the standard approach
Position:	A comfortable, balanced sitting posture.
Procedure:	Presented in forward chaining. Backward chaining also may be used for instruction.

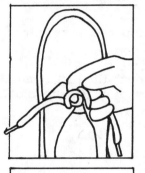

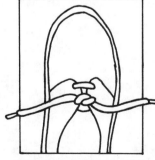

1. Student picks up shoelaces.

2. Student crosses laces across front of shoe.

3. Student puts crossed upper lace under the crossed laces in the triangle created by the laces and shoe.

4. Student grasps lace in each hand and pulls tight.

5. Student repeats step 1.

6. Student repeats step 2.

7. Student repeats step 3.

8. Student grasps upper lace with one hand as it comes through the center of the "knot" without pulling tail through.

9. Student grasps two tails in other hand.

10. Student pulls loop with one hand and tails with the other hand until one loop is tight.

11. Student tucks in tail strings.

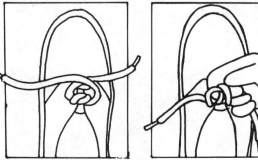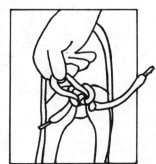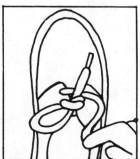

101

ADAPTED TECHNIQUE

Skill: Tie a shoe

Adapted Technique: One string tie hemiplegic method

Materials: Shoe and one shoelace knotted from the inside and laced back and forth straight across the shoe toward the tongue. The end of the shoelace in the last lace hole is toward the *inside* of the shoe, as diagrammed below.

Recommended Student: A hemiplegic student

Position: Sitting, comfortably balanced

Procedure: Presented in forward chaining. Backward chaining also may be used for instruction.

1. Student grasps the shoelace and slips it under the last cross-lacing in a tongue-to-toe direction, pulling it tight, making a loop with it near the tongue.

2. Student holds shoelace tail in a pincer grasp, and makes a loop near the cross-lace, holding the loop.

3. Student puts that loop toward self through the first created loop, and pulls tight in a back-and-forth motion in a slip-knot.

4. Student tucks the shoelace tail in edge of shoe.

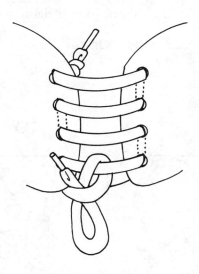

1. List the developmental sequence for buttons, zippers, snaps, buckles, and ties.

2. Describe the standard technique for:
   Buttoning and unbuttoning
   Zipping and unzipping
   Snapping and unsnapping
   Buckling and unbuckling
   Tying and untying

3. Describe three adapted techniques for tying.

Approaches:

1. Be sure the student is balanced comfortably.

2. Sit next to, in front of, or directly behind the student during instruction. Guide the student through the task.

3. Be sure directions are given slowly and clearly.

4. Reinforce the student.

5. Give the student time to succeed.

6. Expect the student to do as much of the task as possible without becoming frustrated.

7. Teach front fasteners first, then side and back fasteners.

8. Be sure fasteners are easy to reach and within the student's vision.

Devices and Hints:

1. To simplify dressing techniques, do without fasteners whenever possible.

2. When buttons, zippers, snaps, and buckles are used, use a size larger than usual.

3. Buttons can be replaced by Velcro. Replace the button with a single Velcro circle. Sew the buttonhole shut and resew the button over the buttonhole. Attach another circle of Velcro to the back of the button.

4. Velcro strips can replace zippers. The Velcro strips can be hidden behind a mock zipper.

5. Reinforce cuff buttons with longer shank threads, or sew them on with elastic thread so the button can remain buttoned while the sleeve is being slipped on or off.

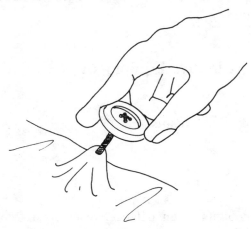

6. Cuff-link cuffs can be put together with two buttons and elastic so they will remain fastened while the hand pushes through the cuff.

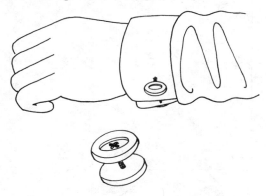

7. Buttons are easier to grasp if they are flat (instead of concave), large, textured, or sewn slightly above the surface of the garment. Be sure buttonholes are large enough for buttoning ease.

8. A safety pin attached to a zipper may make it easier to grasp.

9. A magnetic belt buckle makes buckling easier.

Name eight approaches or devices that can optimize success in fastening and unfastening zippers, buckles, buttons, and snaps.

Adaptive Equipment

Pants

Item: Quad-Quip Trouser Pull

Purpose: To aid in pulling on pants when balance, reach, and fine motor coordination make the task difficult

Socks

Item: Flexible Sock and Stocking Aid

Purpose: To reduce the fine motor control and bending balance usually involved in putting on socks or stockings

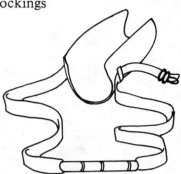

Item: Flexible Sock and Stocking Aid with Cord Handle

Purpose: To reduce the fine motor control and bending balance usually involved in putting on socks or stockings

Item: Deluxe Sock and Stocking Aid

Purpose: To reduce the fine motor control and bending balance usually involved in putting on socks or stockings

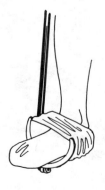

Shoes

Item: Boot/shoe remover (boot jack)

Purpose: To aid in catching heel to remove shoe or boot without having to bend over and grasp heel

Item: Shoe Pet shoehorn

Purpose: To aid in putting on shoe without the balance to reach and bend simultaneously

Item: Be OK Shorty shoehorn

Purpose: To aid in putting on shoe without refined grasp

Item: Plastic shoehorn

Purpose: To aid in putting heel in shoe

Item: Spring action shoehorn

Purpose: To aid in putting on shoe without a refined grasp or balance

Item: Soft, built-up-handled shoehorn

Purpose: Shoehorns come in varying lengths depending on student's needs. The soft, built-up foam handle makes grasp easier.

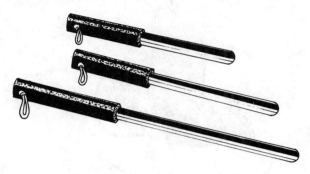

Item: 16" plated shoehorn

Purpose: To aid in putting heel in shoe without stressing balance

Item: Stainless steel shoehorns

Purpose: To aid in putting heel in shoe without stressing balance

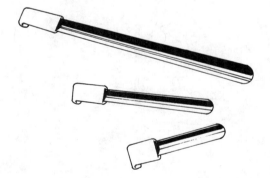

Item: Insert-a-Foot shoe aid

Purpose: To prevent back of shoe from bending as student puts foot in shoe

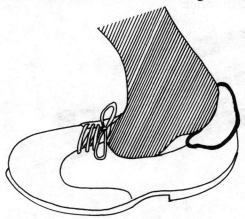

Item: Insert-a-Foot shoe aid with handle

Purpose: To minimize balance stress of bending while preventing back of shoe from bending as student puts on shoe

Buttons

Item: Button aids and Amputee Button Hooks

Purpose: To aid in the fine motor coordination of buttoning

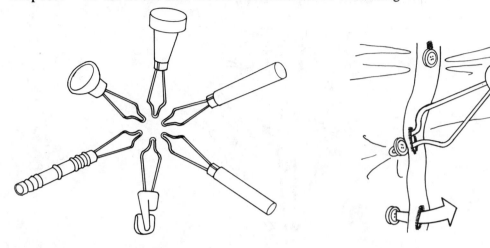

Item: Ball handle button aid

Purpose: To aid in the fine motor coordination of buttoning

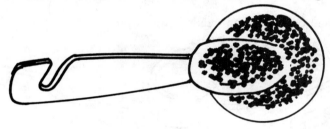

Item: Quad Quip buttoner–zipper pull

Purpose: To aid in the fine motor coordination of buttoning

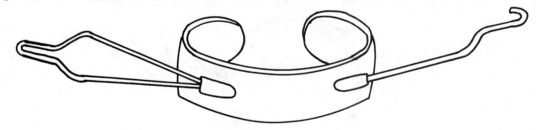

Item: Cuff- and collar-button extender

Purpose: To allow wearer to keep collar or cuff buttoned while dressing

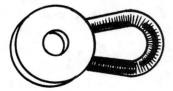

Zippers

Item: Long Reach zipper pull/zipper aid

Purpose: To aid in behind-the-back reaching for zipping

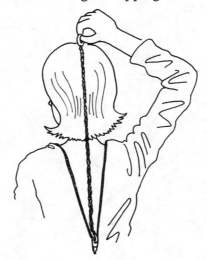

Item: Quad Quip button-zipper pull

Purpose: To aid in the refined coordination needed for zipping

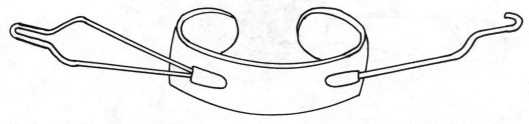

Item: Ring zipper pull

Purpose: To aid in the fine motor coordination needed for pulling zippers

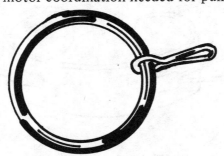

Item: Shorty zipper pull

Purpose: To aid in the fine motor coordination needed for pulling zippers

 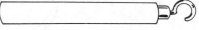

Item: One-handed belt

Purpose: To attach a belt one-handed

Item: Magnetic belt

Purpose: To attach a belt one- or two-handed with less need for refined control

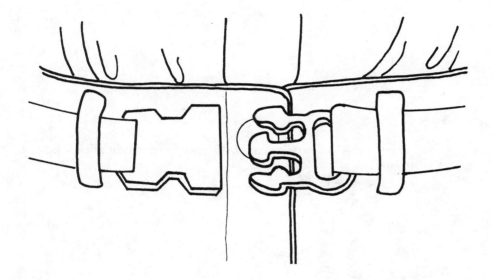

Tying

Item: Tylastic shoelaces

Purpose: Shoes can remain tied while student uses shoehorn to put on shoe. Elastic laces stretch sufficiently to allow independence without untying shoe.

Item: Flex-O-Lace

Purpose: Shoe can be laced prior to putting on with shoehorn. Slide allows laces to be tightened without tying.

Item: Wrap-a-lace shoe fastener

Purpose: To eliminate the fine motor two-handed skill of tying

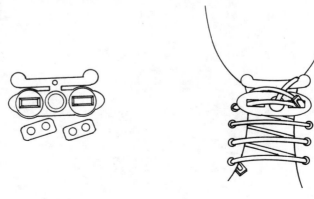

Item: Shoe button

Purpose: To eliminate the fine motor two-handed skill of tying

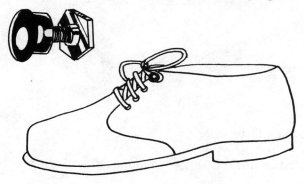

Item: Shoe Lasso

Purpose: To eliminate the fine motor two-handed skill of tying

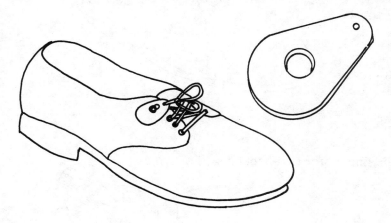

Item: Lacelock

Purpose: To eliminate the fine motor two–handed skill of tying

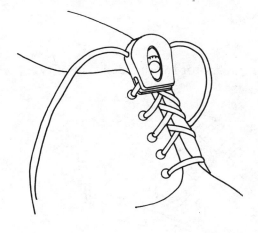

Item: No-Tie stretch lace

Purpose: To eliminate the fine motor two-handed skill of tying

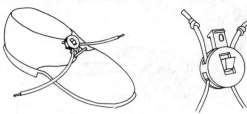

Item: Kno–Bows shoe fasteners

Purpose: To eliminate the fine motor two-handed skill of tying

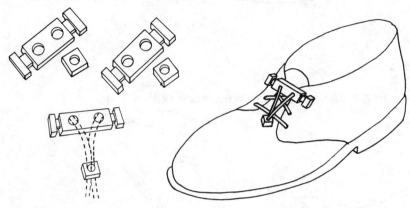

Item: Ortho Lace

Purpose: To eliminate the fine motor two-handed skill of tying

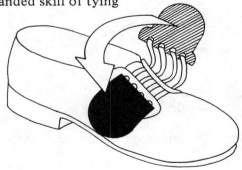

Item: Big D-Ring

Purpose: To eliminate the fine motor two-handed skill of tying

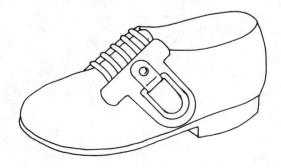

Adaptive Equipment Distributors

AAMED, Inc.
1215 S. Harlem Ave.
Forest Park, IL 60130

Abbey Medical
4826 E. Speedway Blvd.
Tucson, AZ 85712

Achievement Products, Inc.
P.O. Box 547
Mineola, NY 11501

AliMed, Inc.
70 Harrison Ave.
Boston, MA 02111

Cleo Living Aids
3957 Mayfield Road
Cleveland, OH 44121

FashionAble
OT Dept., Drawer S
Rocky Hill, NJ 08553

Functional Fashions by Levis E.P.P.
6621 Geyer Springs Road
Little Rock, AR 72209

Handee for You
Fashions for the Handicapped
7674 Park Ave.
Lowville, NY 13361

Lumex, Inc.
100 Spence St.
Bay Shore, NY 11706

Maddak, Inc.
Industrial Road
Pequannock, NJ 07440

Medical Equipment Distributors (MED)
1701 South First Ave.
Maywood, IL 60153

G. E. Miller
484 S. Broadway
Yonkers, NY 10705

OMED
777 Alpha Drive
Cleveland, OH 44143

PTL Design, Inc.
Box 364
Stillwater, OK 74074

Rehabilitation Equipment, Inc.
2811 Zulette Ave.
Bronx, NY 10461

Rehabilitation Products, Ltd.
4414 Regent St.
Madison, WI 53705

Fred Sammons, Inc.
P.O. Box 32
Brookfield, IL 60513

Special Products for Special People
Everest and Jennings
1803 Pontius Ave.
Los Angeles, CA 90025

Trujillo Industries
5726 W. Washington Blvd.
Los Angeles, CA 90016

Sally Walton
505 E. 116th St.
New York, NY 10029

Western Medical, Inc.
2040 N. 16th St.
Phoenix, AZ 85006

Your Wheelchair Fashions
P.O. Box 99
South Windham, ME 04082

Clothing Construction

1. Be careful to have comfortable fabric near the student's body, so it is not rough or "itchy."

2. Consider fabric that "gives" with movement. Polyester blends tend to resist shrinkage, stretching, and wrinkling while allowing some "give." Jerseys and knits also are easy for dressing and undressing. Acrylic blends are soft, light, warm, and resist wrinkling. Nylon is one of the strongest materials, but in some cases it should be avoided because of its slippery surface.

3. Where necessary, double stitch seams to reinforce areas of stress due to muscle tightness, excessive movement, or bracing.

4. Patch clothing at the knees, hips, and under the arms, to reinforce those areas usually worn through first due to creeping or stress from crutches or braces.

5. Consider whether the garment is constructed in such a way that fasteners can be easily removed or modified as needed.

 List several considerations that should be made regarding construction when selecting clothing.

Clothing Style

1. When purchasing clothing, consider the student's range of motion or joint mobility, and needs for sleeve options, fastener alternatives, neck openings, and fabric considerations.

2. Easy-fit styles are necessary.

3. Avoid tight-fitting clothing. Front opening clothing is helpful when dressing individuals with limited joint mobility.

4. Oversized clothing is helpful for dressing practice, but it may not be appropriate for daily use if it draws attention to the person's dressing skill level or disability.

5. Look for fuller clothing as appropriate.

6. Generally start with larger outer clothing and work inward.

7. Wraparound clothing can be easier for a motorically involved person.

8. Consider sleeve construction for the individual. Raglan and dolman sleeves are easier to get into and out of than set-in sleeves. Short sleeves may be easier than long sleeves.

9. Short jackets or capes or ponchos are easier for the individual in a wheelchair.

 List several considerations that should be made regarding style when selecting clothing.

Resources for Clothing Adaptations

Beerslery, M. C., D. Burns, and J. Weiss. 1977. *Adapt your own: A clothing brochure for people with special needs.* University of Alabama, Division of Continuing Education in Home Economics, P.O. Box 2967, Tuscaloosa, AL.

Bower, M. T. 1977. *Clothing for the handicapped: Fashion adaptations for adults and children.* Sister Kenny Institute, Chicago Avenue at 27th Street, Minneapolis, MN 55407.

Clothing designs for the handicapped. University of Alberta Press, 450 Athabasca Hall, Edmonton, Alberta, Canada T6G 2E8.

Clothing to fit your needs. Iowa State University, Ames, IA 50010.

Convenience clothing and closures. 1975. Talon Ivelcro Consumer Education, 41 E. 51st Street, New York, NY 10022.

Copeland, K., ed. 1974. *Aids for the severely handicapped.* Grune and Stratton, 111 Fifth Avenue, New York, NY 10003.

International Society for Rehabilitation of the Disabled. *Aids for children: Technical aids for physically handicapped children.* International Information Centre on Technical Aids, Fack Street, 161–03, Bromma 3, Sweden.

Hotte, E. B. *Self-help clothing for children who have physical disabilities.* National Easter Seal Society for Crippled Children and Adults, 2023 W. Ogden Avenue, Chicago, IL 60612.

Lowman, E. W., and J. L. Klinger, 1969. *Aids to independent living: Self-help for the handicapped.* McGraw–Hill Book Co., 330 W. 42nd Street, New York, NY 10036.

May, E. E., N. R. Wagonner, and E. B. Hotte. 1974. *Independent living for the handicapped and the elderly.* Houghton Mifflin Co., 110 Fremont Street, Boston, MA 02107.

McCartney, P. 1973. *Clothes sense for handicapped adults of all ages.* Disabled Living Foundation, 346 Kensington High Street, London W14, England.

Wilke, H. H. 1977. *Using everything you've got.* National Easter Seal Society for Crippled Children and Adults, 2023 W. Ogden Avenue, Chicago, IL 60612.

Wilshire, E. R., ed. 1976. *Equipment for the disabled: Clothing and dressing for adults,* 4th ed. Equipment for the Disabled, 2 Foredown Drive, Portslade, Sussex BN4 2BB, England.

Teaching Hemiplegic Students

A hemiplegic person has increased or decreased muscle tone on one side of the body. This asymmetry and muscle imbalance causes special problems in dressing and undressing tasks. Throughout the workbook, adapted techniques and adaptive equipment are described that are specifically intended to maximize independence for the hemiplegic person.

The two general principles to keep in mind in all dressing and undressing procedures for the hemiplegic person are:

1. The affected (weaker) side goes in *first* in dressing.

2. The affected (weaker) side comes out *last* in undressing.

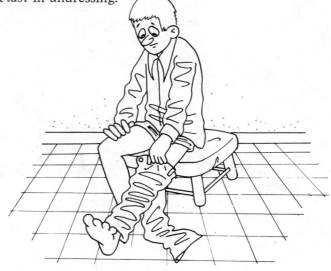

 What are the two principles of dressing and undressing a hemiplegic person?

121

Dressing Students with Cerebral Palsy

Children who have cerebral palsy have the same needs for achieving independence in dressing as do all children. For cerebral palsied children, however, the independence is often more difficult to achieve due to muscle and coordination imbalances and perceptual difficulties.

Individual movement patterns must be considered, but some generalizations can be made for dressing these children.

The children should be in the most relaxed, well-balanced position possible, with minimal environmental distractions and with simple clothing. Children who are spastic often have tight muscle patterns, and then resist movement and changes as they are dressed and undressed. They may stiffen, throw back the head and shoulders, and straighten and cross legs when in a supine position. Their arms may pull tight and bend at the elbow, wrist, and fingers. Athetoid children exhibit different problems because they are in constant motion, with difficulty stabilizing joints to maintain any desired posture, and difficulty moving a part of the body smoothly to assist in the dressing and undressing activities. Some common dressing problems and possible solutions are outlined below.

Problem: Child becomes stiff, legs straight and crossed and head and shoulders back when lying on back, making dressing difficult.

Solution options: The cerebral palsied child becomes stiff due to muscle spasticity and abnormal reflex involvement. To relax tightness:

a. Position the head forward
b. Position the head symmetrically at midline
c. Bend the hips
d. Avoid stimulating the back or back of the head.

Lying on Side

In this position, the child can watch the dress process and can participate as much as possible.

1. The sidelying position with hips bent makes it easier to bring head and shoulders forward to further relax the child.

2. Roll the child side to side during dressing and undressing. The constant slow rolling motion can minimize the chance of the child stiffening while on the back.

Lying Over Your Lap

1. The child is relaxed because no stimulation is made to the back.

2. The child's head and shoulders are forward and hips are bent.

3. The child is symmetrical.

4. Your legs can be slightly apart to keep the child in an easy position for dressing.

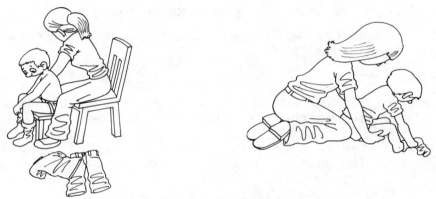

Symmetrical Supported Sitting

In this position, the child can see what is happening in the dressing process and can participate as much as motorically possible.

1. Hold the child's hips bent, head forward at midline, shoulders and trunk forward.

2. Seat the child on your lap or on a firm surface.

Problem:	It is difficult to bend the child's legs to cross them or to put on a shoe.
Solution option:	Bend the child at the hips by pushing up under the big toe, and crossing the leg by bending the hip and knee outward.

Problem:	One side of the child's body is stiffer than the other.
Solution options:	1. Follow the principles stated in "Dressing the Hemiplegic Student."

The stiffer arm or leg goes *in* the clothing first.

The stiffer arm or leg comes *out* last.

2. Have the child positioned in a maximally relaxing posture as described above (lying on side, over your lap, or seated symmetrically).

Problem:	It is difficult to get the child's bent arm through a sleeve.
Solution options:	1. Position the child in a relaxed position with head at midline.

2. Put most affected arm in first.

3. Straighten the child's arm, then put the sleeve *on* rather than pulling arm *in* or grasping the fingers and pulling.

4. If the child's fingers tend to get caught, try putting a mitten over the hand.

Problem:	The child stiffens when approached for dressing or undressing with unexpected noise or movement.
Solution options:	Cerebral palsied persons often have difficulty isolating their responses. They tend to react with total body tension to some visual, auditory, tactile, and movement stimuli.

1. Be sure the child is in a relaxed position.

2. Tell the child what you are about to do.

3. Approach the child slowly from within vision.

Problem:	The child's toes curl, making it difficult to get the toes straight in the shoe.
Solution options:	1. Have the child in a relaxed position, sitting symmetrically, head at midline. Cross the leg being dressed.

2. Try using shoes that unlace completely to the toe so the foot can be placed in the shoe.

3. Consider shoes with cut-out or clear toes so you can see the toes in the shoe.

4. See "Adaptive Equipment: Shoes" (page 108).

Problem: What should we teach cerebral palsied children who are working on *independence* in dressing?

Solution options:

1. They need to be taught the same techniques, to maximally stabilize and relax themselves, that were given above for dressing a child.

2. Sidelying is a good position, to avoid the need for sitting balance.

3. Use walls and corners for support.

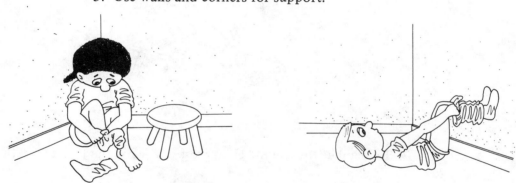

4. Use chairs or grab bars as needed for support.

5. To improve balance, have the child sit with feet flat on the floor, holding behind with one or two hands. This helps the child sit straighter during the dressing process. Keeping one hand on the stool while the other dresses can give added balance.

6. Have the child sit on a bench or stool with the trunk *rotated* to help relaxation.

7. Remember to have the child cross one leg if the toes curl in the shoe.

8. A small wooden box can provide extra balance for the hemiplegic cerebral palsied child.

9. Use a bed or chair for support in kneeling.

1. List five positions or handling techniques to make it easier to dress the cerebral palsied child.

2. List three positions that may allow more independence for the cerebral palsied child who is learning self-dressing.

Teaching Blind Students

Close your eyes, then dress yourself. You'll begin to understand the difficulties encountered by blind people when they are learning a new sequential task. (Trying to simulate *any* disability — whether it be blindness, hemiplegia, arthritis, or other motoric imbalance — can help the instructor understand the modifications which must be made in teaching approaches or techniques so these students can succeed.)

If you did close your eyes and put on a shirt, you probably would notice that your approach to dressing was a standard one with extra difficulty in orientation of the shirt and aligning buttons. Blind students generally follow the developmental sequences described for all children, with extra time needed for fasteners and orientation of clothing articles.

The following points address these issues for instruction of dressing with blind students:

1. Start dressing and undressing instruction early by establishing a routine.
2. Do each task the same way each time so the sequence is predictable for the student.
3. Talk about what you are doing, while you are doing it.
4. Pause during the process so the student can anticipate the next step of the process and become an active participant.
5. Use simple clothing to reduce confusion.
6. Allow the student enough time to react.
7. Label the inside back of each article of clothing with safety pins or textured tags so the student has an easier time with orientation. In this area the blind student frequently needs extra assistance.
8. Colors can be coded by a tactile marking system to aid the child in selecting color-coordinated outfits.
9. Help student select clothing by texture.
10. Zippers and elastic waistbands tend to be easier for the blind student than buttons.
11. Blind students often like hats that cover their ears. However, these can interfere with the students' ability to locate themselves.
12. Clothing should be kept in an orderly fashion. Drawers should be neat. The students should have a particular plan for putting away clothing as it is taken off, so they can find it easily.

List eight approaches for teaching dressing to a blind student.

Classroom Pre-Dressing Activities

The following pages outline activities that help the learner develop dressing skills. They can be prepared easily for classroom use.

These are only some of the activities that could be used to vary the teaching of dressing skills. They are meant to stimulate your creativity. At the end of this section, a blank activity sheet is included. You may reproduce that form as often as necessary, for administrative use.

Superheroes

Purpose: To have fun with dressing practice

Skill stage: All stages

Materials: Superhero costumes (Batman, Robin Hood, Star Wars characters, Wonder Woman, Superman)

Position: All positions

Procedure:
1. Have the children select the "superhero" costume they would like to wear.

2. Have them find all the parts to their costume from a pile of costumes.

3. Have the children put on their costume and have fun pretending to be the superhero.

Holiday Costumes

Purpose: To have fun with dressing and undressing practice

Skill stage: Any or all skill stages

Materials: Costumes representing holidays (Valentine's Day Cupids, St. Patrick's Day leprechauns, Thanksgiving Pilgrims, Christmas Santas, and so on)

Position: All positions

Procedure: The children can use or make costumes to dress up for holiday parades or plays.

Doll Dress-Up

Purpose: To practice dressing and undressing skills with dolls

Skill stage: Dressing and undressing shirts, dresses, pants, and fastening fasteners

Materials: Dolls and dress-up clothes

Position: Sitting

Procedure: Have the children play dress-up with dolls. They can dress and undress the doll completely or can practice with only one article of clothing repeatedly.

Musical Dressing

Purpose: To put on different articles of clothing while listening to music and interacting with other children

Skill stage: Dressing and undressing; fastening and unfastening

Materials: Dress-up clothing

Position: Any position

Procedure: This is a variation of Musical Chairs. The children reach into a center pile of clothing and put on articles of dress while the music is playing. They stop the activity when the music stops. The winner is the student with the most clothing on when the music stops.

Smock Games

Purpose: To put on smocks or aprons during classroom activity

Skill stage: Dressing and undressing shirts; fastening and unfastening buttons, snaps, or ties

Materials: Smocks or aprons with a variety of fasteners

Procedure: The students practice putting on and taking off shirts and fastening fasteners while putting on smocks for classroom water play, cooking activities, sand activities, finger painting, and so on. Dressing can be integrated into the daily routine purposively this way, rather than being purely an "exercise."

Button Boards

Purpose: To practice buttoning in a sequence

Skill stage: Buttoning and unbuttoning

Materials: Purchased or homemade button boards

Position: All positions

Variations: Zip boards, buckle boards, tie boards, snap boards

Procedure: Have the students manipulate boards to fasten and unfasten fasteners

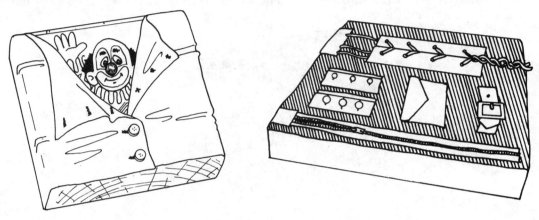

Cloth Button Book

Purpose: To learn and practice unbuttoning and buttoning

Skill stage: Unbuttoning and buttoning

Materials: Purchased or homemade button books

Position: Sitting, prone on elbows, standing, kneeling

Procedure: Children practice unbuttoning and buttoning picture parts on cloth pages

Matching Sock Game

Purpose: To practice putting on and taking off socks while interacting in a group activity

Skill stage: Socks on and off

Materials: A number of pairs of socks in all sizes, textures, and colors

Position: All positions

Procedure:
1. The children sit in a circle. There are a number of pairs of socks in the center of the circle.

2. At the sound of the whistle, the children race to find a matching pair of socks and be the first to put them on.

3. Then the child can try to be the first to take off the socks.

Variation: Big Shoe Race

Purpose: To practice matching, lacing, putting on, and tying shoes

Skill stage: Lacing and tying shoes

Position: Standing and sitting

Procedure:
1. Place a pile of shoes in the center of a group of children. The pile has one shoe from each pair.

2. Each child is given one shoe.

3. At the sound of the bell, the children try to find the shoe in the pile that matches the one they were given.

4. The children then lace and tie the shoe as quickly as possible.

Wooden Shoe Box

Purpose: To practice tying on a stationary shoe box
(In this activity, tying is closer to the body than tying on the foot, and in an easier perspective than on a shirt, dress, or apron.)

Skill stage: Tying shoes

Materials: A wooden shoe box

Position: Comfortably balanced, usually sitting

Procedure: The children can sit at a table or on the floor to practice tying the shoe. They can also participate in shoe-tying relays with each other.

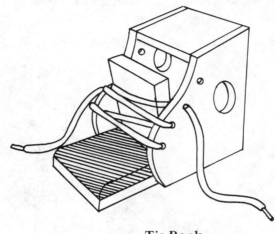

Tie Book

Purpose: To practice tying on a tie book
(In this activity, tying is closer to the body than tying on a foot, and in an easier perspective than on a shirt, dress, or apron.)

Skill stage: Tying

Materials: Purchased or homemade tie books

Position: Comfortably balanced, usually sitting

Procedure: Have the children practice untying and tying bows in a "Bow" book. The book can contain ribbons only; or each "bow" picture can be a different article of clothing decorated by a bow (for example, a girl's face with a bow in her hair, a boy wearing a bow tie, an apron with apron strings, a shoe with a bow).

Package Wrapping

Purpose: To wrap packages as a way to practice tying

Skill stage: Tying

Materials: Packages of different sizes; a variety of different textured and thicknesses of wrapping, ribbons, yarns, or ropes

Position: Any posture that is comfortable

Procedure: 1. Have the student wrap packages and tie bows for various occasions.

2. Each child can have a "work box." Every day they untie the box, take out their work, then put it away and retie the box.

Apron Tie

Purpose: To practice tying and untying during daily playtime

Skill stage: Tying

Materials: Aprons in a variety of sizes and shapes

Position: Standing

Procedure: Create times during the day for the children to practice tying knots and bows. Have them put on tie-aprons or smocks before finger painting and easel activities, waterplay, or cooking activities.

Wooden Lace Boards

Purpose: To practice lacing shoelaces through holes

Skill stage: Lacing shoes

Materials: Wooden lace boards made of fiberboard
(Glue a picture on the board to increase the child's interest.)

Position: Sitting, kneeling, half-kneeling, standing

Procedure: Have the student lace the board in a variety of designated patterns.

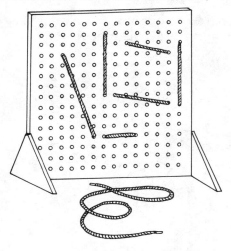

Cardboard Lace Cards

Purpose: To practice lacing shoelaces through holes

Skill stage: Lacing shoes

Materials: Paper plates, shoelaces, staples, pictures, bells

Position: Sitting comfortably

Procedure: Punch holes around a paper plate. Have the student lace around the edge.

Variation: Have the student lace two plates together with beads or bells inside to make a rhythm shaker.

CLASSROOM PRE-DRESSING ACTIVITY

PURPOSE:

SKILL STAGE:

MATERIALS:

POSITION:

PROCEDURES:

VARIATION:

Weekly Activity Planning

Now you know how to assess pre-dressing skills and choose sequential goals and methods. You also have some ideas about different clothing sizes, textures, and styles that can maximize student success. It is important in a classroom to plan a week of activities that allow the students to practice the pre-dressing skills in a variety of ways and at appropriate times.

A sample "Weekly Pre-Dressing Activity Plan" follows, and a blank activity plan form is given on page 140. You may reproduce this form as often as necessary for administrative use.

Choose a pre-dressing skill stage of development, and think of how many ways you can teach that behavior.

SAMPLE WEEKLY PRE-DRESSING ACTIVITY PLAN

Student: _Anita_

Week: _June 8-12_

Objective: _To button a large button_

Day	Activity	Time	Position
Monday	Put on a front-button smock	Before finger painting	Sit
Tuesday	Button a doll shirt	Midmorning	Squat Kneel
Wednesday	Put together a button board	Midmorning	Sit
Thursday	Do button relay	After lunch	Stand
Friday	Put on a front-button smock	Before cooking activity	Stand at a mirror

WEEKLY PRE-DRESSING ACTIVITY PLAN

Student: _____

Week: _____

Objective: _____

Day	Activity	Time	Position
Monday			
Tuesday			
Wednesday			
Thursday			
Friday			

Planning an Individual Pre-Dressing Program

It is important in classroom or therapy settings to set up a long-range instruction plan for the individual student. Whether you develop an informal program or a formal written program to meet Federal, state, local, or personal standards, the following factors should be considered.

1. **Developmental pre-dressing skills.** What pre-dressing skills does the learner exhibit? What is the learner's current level of performance? At what stage does the pre-dressing checklist show the student to be succeeding? Clearly indicate what the learner can and cannot do in pre-dressing tasks. Are there any motoric or sensory limitations that affect pre-dressing skills?

2. **Long-term goals.** What is a realistic long-term expectation for this learner? Do you expect total independence in dressing, adapted independence, partial independence, or to maximize the learner's involvement to promote ease by the caregiver in dressing the learner?

3. **Sequential objective.** What is the specific next behavior to be learned? Due to the varied nature of dressing skills, there may be several skills being taught simultaneously (for example, socks off, shoes off, shirt off). Is this sequential objective learnable? Is it broken down into enough steps so that the learner can succeed? Does the learner have the sensory and motor skills required in behavioral terms that can be measured? What is the criterion for success? How often does the task need to be performed successfully in order for the student to advance to the next step? It is important to write this objective specifically in order to document progress and to help the student succeed.

4. **Equipment and materials.** What clothing will be used to maximize success? Will it be adapted clothing, or clothing that is too big? Will it be of a certain texture or color to promote success? Is adaptive equipment needed? Will the adaptive equipment be phased out, or is it to be used long-term?

5. **Position.** What position will be used to teach this pre-dressing skill? What position offers sufficient support?

6. **Environment.** In what room will the student be when performing this task? Are any special environmental considerations imposed by the person's physical limitations? Are there visual or auditory distractions to be minimized?

7. **Time of day.** At what time of day will this task be presented? What tasks follow or precede this activity? Is there a natural reason to be dressing at that time?

8. **Methodology.** How are you going to teach this pre-dressing skill? Any task analysis should include the following components:
   a. What do you as a teacher do or say to elicit the desired response?
   b. What is the learner expected to do or say in response?
   c. What type of reinforcement will be provided for correct response?
   d. What action will the teacher take if the learner responds incorrectly to the original directions? (Repeat directions? Provide an imitative model? Provide physical assistance?)
   e. How will data be collected?

9. **Maintenance activities.** What activities will the student practice to ensure that the learned skill is maintained? Will the learner be allowed or required to use the skill in daily dressing activities?

INDIVIDUAL PRE-DRESSING PROGRAM

Name: _____

Date: _____ Classroom: _____

DEVELOPMENTAL PRE-DRESSING SKILLS:

LONG-TERM GOALS:

SEQUENTIAL OBJECTIVE:

EQUIPMENT AND MATERIALS:

POSITION:

ENVIRONMENT:

TIME OF DAY:

METHODOLOGY:

MAINTENANCE ACTIVITIES:

DRESSING TASK

SKILL: _____

OBJECTIVE:

APPROXIMATE
DEVELOPMENTAL AGE:

MATERIALS:

POSITION:

TASK ANALYSIS:

ADAPTED TECHNIQUE

SKILL:

ADAPTED TECHNIQUE:

MATERIALS:

RECOMMENDED STUDENT:

POSITION:

PROCEDURE:

Post-Test

1. List four principles of maturation that influence the process of growth and development.

    a.

    b.

    c.

    d.

2. List eight prerequisites for dressing.

    a.

    b.

    c.

    d.

    e.

    f.

    g.

    h.

3. List the sequence strategy for the instruction for dressing, from least restrictive to most restrictive approaches.

    a.

    b.

    c.

    d.

    e.

4. Describe a standard dressing approach for:

   a. Putting on a front-button shirt

   b. Removing a front-button shirt

   c. Putting on a T-shirt

   d. Removing a T-shirt

   e. Putting on pants

   f. Removing pants

   g. Putting on shoes

   h. Removing shoes

   i. Putting on socks

   j. Removing socks

   k. Buttoning

   l. Unbuttoning

   m. Zipping

n. Unzipping

o. Snapping

p. Unsnapping

q. Buckling

r. Unbuckling

s. Tying

t. Untying

5. Describe an adapted dressing approach for:

a. Putting on a front-button shirt

b. Removing a front-button shirt

c. Putting on a T-shirt

d. Removing a T-shirt

e. Putting on pants

f. Removing pants

g. Putting on shoes

h. Removing shoes

i. Putting on socks

j. Removing socks

k. Tying

6. List an adaptive device for:

a. Pants

b. Shirts

c. Shoes

d. Socks

e. Fasteners

7. List a commercially available piece of adaptive equipment used to aid in independence in:

a. Putting on pants

b. Putting on shoes

c. Tying shoes

d. Buttoning

e. Zipping

f. Buckling

8. Describe the teaching approach of backward chaining.

9. Describe the teaching approach of forward chaining.

10. List two dressing approaches, considerations, or hints for teaching:

   a. Shirts

   b. Pants

   c. Shoes

   d. Socks

   e. Fasteners

11. List two principles of dressing and undressing for the hemiplegic student.

    a.

    b.

12. List six handling or positioning techniques that can be helpful in relaxing or stabilizing the cerebral palsied student during dressing.

    a.

    b.

    c.

    d.

    e.

    f.

13. List five principles of dressing and undressing for the blind student.

    a.

    b.

    c.

d.

e.

14. List two construction considerations to be made in choosing clothing.

    a.

    b.

15. List two style considerations to be made in choosing clothing.

    a.

    b.

16. List five classroom pre-dressing activities.

    a.

    b.

    c.

    d.

    e.

17. List the components in an Individual Pre-Dressing Program.

References

Baldwin, L., and H. D. Fredricks. 1976. *Isn't it time he outgrew this? Or: A training program for parents of retarded children.* Springfield, IL: Charles B. Thomas Publishers.

Brown, D., V. Simmons, and J. Methvin. 1978. *The Oregon project for visually impaired and blind preschool children.* Medford, OR: Jackson County Education Service District.

California State Department of Education. 1976. *Learning steps.* Sacramento, CA: California State Department of Education.

Coley, I. L. 1978. *Pediatric assessment of self-care activities.* St. Louis: C. V. Mosby Company.

Finnie, N. R. 1974. *Handling the young cerebral palsied child at home.* New York: E. P. Dutton.

Hofmeister, A. M., and M. Gallery, 1977. *Training for independence: A program for teaching the independent use of zippers, buttons, shoes, and socks.* Niles, IL: Developmental Learning Materials.

Hofmeister, A. M., and J. Hofmeister. 1977. *Training for independent dressing skills.* Niles, IL: Developmental Learning Materials.

Hotte, E. B. 1979. *Self-help clothing.* Chicago, IL: National Easter Seal Society for Crippled Children and Adults.

Levitt, S. 1982. *Treatment of cerebral palsy and motor delay.* St. Louis: Blackwell Mosby Book Distributors.

Lindford, M., L. W. Hipsher, and R. G. Silikovitz. 1972. *Systematic instruction for retarded children: The Illinois program.* Danville, IL: Interstate Printers & Publishers, Inc.

Lowman, E. W. 1959. *Self-help devices for the arthritic.* New York: Institute of Physical Medicine and Rehabilitation of New York University.

Morrison, D., P. Pothier, and K. Horr. 1978. *Sensory motor dysfunction and therapy in infancy and early childhood.* Springfield, IL: Charles Thomas.

Perkins School for the Blind. 1976. *Curriculum for daily living.* Boston: New England Regional Center for Services of Deaf-Blind Children.

Scott, E. P. 1977. *Can't your child see?* Baltimore: University Park Press.

Trombly, C. A. 1977. *Occupational therapy for physical dysfunction.* Baltimore: Williams & Wilkins Co.

Umbreit, J., and P. J. Cardullias. 1980. *Curriculum adaptations.* Columbus, OH: Special Press.

Yeadon, A. 1978. *Toward independence.* New York: American Foundation for the Blind.